W9-AJM-013

ven
pb

**Project Manager/Writer:** Wanda J. Ventling
**Senior Associate Design Director:** Ken Carlson
**Contributing Writer:** Jilann Severson
**Copy Chief:** Terri Fredrickson
**Publishing Operations Manager:** Karen Schirm
**Edit and Design Production Coordinator:** Mary Lee Gavin
**Editorial Assistants:** Kaye Chabot, Kairee Windsor
**Marketing Product Managers:** Aparna Pande, Isaac Petersen, Gina Rickert, Stephen Rogers, Brent Wiersma, Tyler Woods
**Book Production Managers:** Pam Kvitne, Marjorie J. Schenkelberg, Rick von Holdt, Mark Weaver
**Contributing Copy Editor:** Jane Woychick
**Contributing Proofreaders:** Becky Etchen, Beth Havey, Nancy Ruhling
**Contributing Photographers:** George Lange, Paul Whicheloe (Anyway Productions Inc.)
**Indexer:** Sharon Duffy

**Meredith Books**
**Executive Director, Editorial:** Gregory H. Kayko
**Executive Director, Design:** Matt Strelecki
**Senior Editor/Group Manager:** Vicki L. Ingham

**Publisher and Editor in Chief:** James D. Blume
**Editorial Director:** Linda Raglan Cunningham
**Executive Director, Marketing:** Jeffrey B. Myers
**Executive Director, New Business Development:** Todd M. Davis
**Executive Director, Sales:** Ken Zagor
**Director, Operations:** George A. Susral
**Director, Production:** Douglas M. Johnston
**Business Director:** Jim Leonard

**Vice President and General Manager:** Douglas J. Guendel

**Meredith Publishing Group**
**President:** Jack Griffin
**Senior Vice President:** Bob Mate

**Meredith Corporation**
**Chairman and Chief Executive Officer:** William T. Kerr
**President and Chief Operating Officer:** Stephen M. Lacy

**In Memoriam:** E.T. Meredith III (1933-2003)

**While You Were Out Book Development Team**
Roger Marmet, Executive Vice President and General Manager, TLC
Michael Klein, Executive Producer, TLC
Abigail Harvey, Executive Producer, BBC NY Productions
Sara Kozak, Series Producer, BBC NY Productions
Sharon M. Bennett, Senior Vice President, Discovery Global Licensing
Carol LeBlanc, Vice President, Marketing & Retail Development
Elizabeth Bakacs, Vice President, Creative Resources, Global Licensing
Erica Jacobs Green, Director of Publishing
Cheryl King, Publishing Associate

# While
## you were
# out

Meredith® Books
Des Moines, Iowa

# Contents

# 52 The Rooms

See how 13 dreams come true and learn how you can adapt creative decorating and design ideas to your own home.

# The
# show

# The talented *While You Were Out* team touches lives and transforms spaces, proving to surprised homeowners that dreams really do come true.

*hile You Were Out* is a high-energy, interior design reality series with a big heart. Each episode features a remarkable 48-hour room makeover filled with design solutions, interesting projects, and low-cost decorating ideas put together by a creative team of hardworking professionals on a $1,500 budget. This show offers more than amazing interior design; it's also an opportunity for participants to give a loved one a brand-new room and the surprise of a lifetime.

The idea is simple. A family member, friend, or co-worker decides to surprise a special someone with a fantasy room makeover and contacts *While You Were Out* to apply to be on the show. Because the show depends so heavily on the element of surprise, the most important qualification for any applicant is

secrecy: The person who will receive the room makeover must not know about the application.

After an applicant is selected, secrecy must continue throughout the screening and production process, or the makeover is canceled. Although it's a challenge at times, keeping the secret until the end, when the completed room is revealed, ensures a surprise ending for all involved.

When selecting applicants, *While You Were Out* recruiters look for passionate homeowners to excite and test the designers. They prefer spaces that present challenges and even ask for eccentric or wild design fantasies and rooms with strong, dramatic themes. Their primary goal is to capture for the television audience a fabulous makeover, a compelling story, and people who are fun to watch.

After the initial screening process, the applications are narrowed down to a few finalists. The lucky ones who make it this far are contacted, and a scout visits each home. At that time each applicant is interviewed in person, and the location logistics are considered. For the designers, the scout gathers structural information and takes various room measurements, photos, and a videotape.

After the scout reports back with the details, the final decision is made. If the room is approved, a date is set for the makeover. Plans are also made for getting the "away partner" out of town for the days of the makeover and filming. This usually involves arranging a trip with a friend or family member who is wise to the scheme. The accomplice keeps tabs on the homeowner and reports back to the *While You Were Out* team.

About two to three weeks before taping the show, the designers get briefed on the details of the room, see the scouting materials, and learn about the people involved. The designers have their own individual routines, but generally they develop a design plan with fabric and project-material samples. The design plan includes a floor plan, elevation drawings, and project sketches with dimensions and specifications.

The designers purchase most of the materials and ready-made items and have them shipped in advance to the hotel where the crew will be staying. This gives them the opportunity to shop at their favorite designer haunts in New York, Los Angeles, and other major cities, where they often can get some great bargains. Items generally available throughout the country, such as wood, hardware, and basic sewing and crafts supplies, are purchased locally the day before the makeover begins.

The designers also select prizes—special items that work with the room design. These range from small decorative objects such as a vintage martini set to a large leather sofa. A baby grand piano and an original painting were two of the most expensive prizes ever given, each more than $6,000.

Each episode features three prizes, which the homeowner gets to keep if all goes well. During the makeover the person who applied to be on the show must correctly answer two questions. After the room is revealed, the surprised partner is asked a final question. If he or she doesn't answer correctly, the last prize will be lost—one important item from the room.

# The Countdown

**Day 0** (The day before the makeover) The day starts with a planning meeting to discuss the overall design and projects, shopping lists, and items shipped. After the meeting, the team makes a brief, covert visit to the home site to see the room in person for the first time. The afternoon is spent shopping at local stores and home improvement centers.

**Day 1** The team arrives at the site. After cast members get their microphones and makeup on, they begin filming. The design plan is revealed, the trucks are unloaded, and the day gets under way.

**Day 2** The team arrives at the site before breakfast. Then it's a race to the finish to get the room done and get all the sets broken down and loaded onto the trailer before the reveal.

# The Secret Shooter

One person intended to stay out of the limelight is the secret shooter, a cameraperson whose assignment is to film the homeowner while he or she is out of town. Usually the filming is done under the guise of making a tourist or promotional video, or the shooter offers some other plausible reason for wanting to tape.

In a few instances the secret shooter has been caught, such as during the filming of Episode 248, "Palm Tree Paradise." While away, the homeowner saw a commercial for *While You Were Out* and recognized the silhouette and voice of the cameraman as the same person who was filming him for a "tourism tape." Even though the shooter was busted, the design of the room was a hit.

To date, the secret shooter has been caught only three times. If a homeowner does get suspicious, it's usually for other reasons, such as when a local radio station announced that the show was in town. But even if the homeowner gets wise before the reveal, the room design is always a surprise.

Homeowner Jack Raleigh Jr. knew something was up when he saw and heard his secret shooter on television!

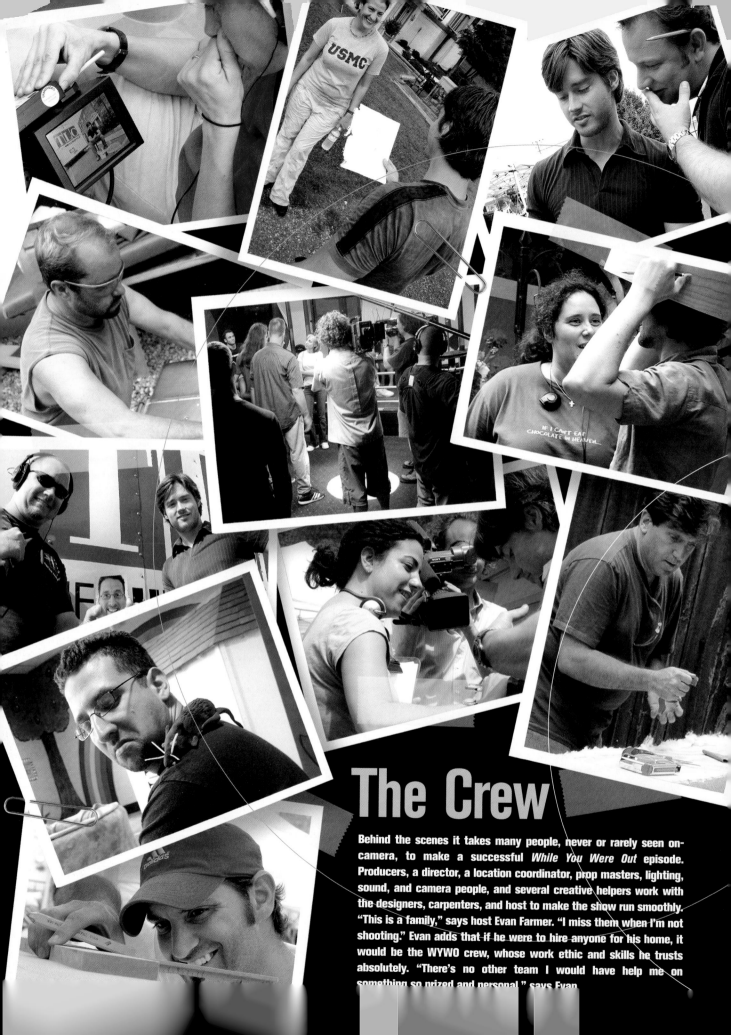

# The Crew

Behind the scenes it takes many people, never or rarely seen on-camera, to make a successful *While You Were Out* episode. Producers, a director, a location coordinator, prop masters, lighting, sound, and camera people, and several creative helpers work with the designers, carpenters, and host to make the show run smoothly. "This is a family," says host Evan Farmer. "I miss them when I'm not shooting." Evan adds that if he were to hire anyone for his home, it would be the WYWO crew, whose work ethic and skills he trusts absolutely. "There's no other team I would have help me on something so prized and personal," says Evan.

# The Quiz

Being the resident quizmaster, host Evan Farmer brainstorms with *While You Were Out* associate producers to come up with good questions and a selection of answers. The associate producers have to have done their homework to learn all about the "away" partner. They use that information to make up the questions. "Some of the most laughs we have are sitting around coming up with quiz answer alternatives. I look forward to the quizzes since it's an off-the-record laughfest that knows no bounds," says Evan.

# The Set

Traveling with enough tools and equipment to transform any given room within 48 hours is a challenge, especially when the *While You Were Out* team is on the road about nine months of the year. The trailer is critical to the show's success. It carries a full array of carpentry and woodworking tools and equipment, a complete sewing setup, and bins filled with supplies of paper towels, paint tarps, brushes and rollers, gloves, nails, screws, and all the other small items needed to redecorate a room. Two efficient prop masters travel with the trailer and keep it organized and well-stocked.

A design show this challenging takes an experienced team who can run with the ball— and punt when needed—to win the game.

# The
# Cast

# Host Evan Farmer

## Blending in with the crowd was Evan Farmer's desire as a kid. Now he shows his stuff as the outgoing, live-wire host of *While You Were Out.*

When the camera turns on Evan Farmer, it's like watching Clark Kent metamorphose into Superman. One minute he's a reserved man talking about financial investments, his renovation business that's revitalizing apartments, or his love for his family. The next minute, with the camera rolling, he is instantly energized, ready with his own brand of well-timed physical comedy, subtle comebacks, and a willingness to be the butt of a joke for the sake of a laugh.

As part of his job, Evan served as a target for a police dog, sat fully clothed in 6-inch-deep water after a rainstorm, bathed in a homeowner's bathtub on-camera, and built carpentry projects wearing a grass skirt. All this, and much more, from a guy who until recently wouldn't even wear red.

"I've always aspired to come out of my shell. I was very conservative growing up. I would wear white if white would blend, green if green would blend," says Evan. But he's self-reflective and says he makes improvements where there's a need. He now wears red on the advice of a friend, even though it makes him "extremely uncomfortable." Not an expected challenge for a guy who was the opening act for Britney Spears during her 2000 *Oops!...I Did It Again* summer tour, but Evan Farmer is a complex guy.

He was born in Ethiopia, where his father served in the U.S. Army Medic Corps. Spending much of his childhood traveling the world, Evan and his family eventually settled in Baltimore, where he attended high school.

"After high school I was accepted into and attended the Tulane School of Architecture for two years," he says. But working in architects' offices during the summer made him change his mind. "I loved architecture school. I hated the reality of working in architecture as a profession . . . I was in desperate need of a less restrictive outlet for my creativity," says Evan. He started working in television commercials about this time and mixed that with playing in rock bands and working in occasional theater projects. Ultimately he graduated with a degree in organizational issues management. Later Evan worked as both a draftsman and a graphic designer for several firms while pursuing other creative outlets.

"Basically my search has always been for a way to be myself, be creative, and still feed myself," says Evan. "Postcollege I went to New York City where I bartended in between soap gigs, toured Russia with Na-Na (a popular rock band), and eventually ended up off-Broadway in *The Fantastiks*. "That's when I got my first of a series of

# The Evan Farmer Quiz

**1) When asked what his favorite design style is, did Evan say:**

A) I love country blue and mauve...and my plaster of Paris cat collection!

B) I am a minimalist, so I have everything in gray. In time, I'd like a red pillow.

C) My favorite style is function defining form.

**2) When asked what trend he'd like to start, did Evan say:**

A) A trend of wearing shirts with different phrases and words on them.

B) A trend of accountability—to challenge others to do something great.

C) A trend of not following trends.

**3) When asked what about the show makes him most proud, did Evan say:**

A) The fact that entire families watch our show together.

B) The fact that we don't have unlimited funds to do the projects.

C) That this is reality television and we even show our mistakes.

films that led me to Vancouver, L.A., and television," he explains.

His small-screen credits include starring roles in a television series and a recurring role on a soap opera. Evan also lent his voice to a popular animated comedy series for three years.

He'd just returned to New York City after several out-of-state jobs and had planned to record his first solo album, when he was asked to join *While You Were Out* as the host.

"*While You Were Out* was the right job at the right time with the right elements," he says. "My experiences on a whole led me back to the ultimate mix of entertainment and design. I could not be happier!" And in his spare time he now continues with his music interests and maintains other creative projects.

"I really didn't prepare for this job specifically, though it was certainly an ideal fit for me considering my entirely nonlinear path of experiences and interests," says Evan. "The fact that I've been all over the place and have done all kinds of things in all parts of the world allows me to bring a perspective that hopefully bridges the gap between the millions of people who may be watching at any given time," he says.

While the show lets Evan explore his natural talent as host, it also offers him an opportunity to express his love for architecture and design. "What I love to do ultimately is to find creative solutions to problems. I'm very much a typical guy in the respect

that I like to solve stuff. It's a passion." His skills are appreciated by the others. "The designers have learned they can hand over projects to me that haven't been totally engineered, and I can usually come up with something," Evan says. "If there's a tough project, I won't sleep until I've figured it out."

He's transferred what he's learned to design his own place too. "I am taking a very small space and turning it into an interactive, multifunctional, New York apartment, which will probably end up resembling the inside of my brain...sort of," he says. "Every item will, and must, have at least two functions."

"The fact that this show requires us to solve design problems in an extremely short period of time is exactly what makes me feel complete at the end of the day," says Evan. "We're very much inventors."

He is proud that families can watch *While You Were Out* as a group. "I meet whole families, kids through grandparents, who watch the show together. That's a positive change in my opinion, from the fragmented television [programming] that requires every member of a family to have a separate television [set]. Some of my fondest memories growing up were sitting together with my family watching Donny and Marie Osmond, Sonny and Cher, or listening to *A Prairie Home Companion* on the radio," he says. "I'd like to think we're a part of bringing that aspect back to television."

**"It's basically a race** to the finish, getting as much done as possible."

# Designer John Bruce

**Designer John Bruce creates contemporary spaces with good vibes. He is known for his inventive use of materials, cutting-edge lighting, and uncanny ability to be cool.**

t is 9:30 a.m. on what promises to be a slow-cook day in southern Florida. For John Bruce, it is Day Zero. Dressed in heavy black shoes, loose-fitting jeans and a T-shirt, he has his signature satchel slung across his slight frame and carries a long cardboard tube filled with specialty art papers in his hand. He is a soulful, unassuming man who entertains and communicates with his eyes.

"I'm told I look very serious, even though I'm probably one of the silliest people I know," says John. "I'm a bit of a page torn from a book. Once I'm found out, I will be rightly asked to leave the party."

John has a track record as a successful filmmaker, with work that includes a public television documentary and countless music videos. He admits he is happiest working behind the camera and never intended or desired to be in front of it. Yet when asked to join the *While You Were Out* design team, he was intrigued. "It was like a job had been invented that matched what I had already been doing. *While You Were Out* isn't merely interior decorating—it's more like installation art and experimental theater on a downtown budget," he says.

Today is a typical workday for John as he surveys for the first time the cramped, overstuffed room, complicated by walls of windows, merging traffic patterns, and mixed flooring. He is expected to head a small team of creative professionals as he does for every show; this time carpenters Jason Cameron and Ali Barone will assist in transforming the space on camera in 48 hours. "I've done 28 of these shows but it doesn't get any easier or quicker. The show is always challenging," he says. "Each time I have to dig deeper."

Most professional designers would turn and run, scared at the magnitude of the task, but John unloads the satchel and tube onto the sofa, stares in wonderment at the room for a few minutes, and begins measuring the walls. The narrow, L-shape living space is a jumble of spent furniture and unrelated castoff accessories. There are stacks of papers and several pillows taking up most of the space on the little sofa, which is pressed snugly against a wall-size arched window.

"There are so many considerations to account for in a *While You Were Out* episode; so many simultaneous options and restrictions. It's this giant thing that needs to be navigated down to a pinpoint target," he explains, "like landing a jumbo jet in your backyard."

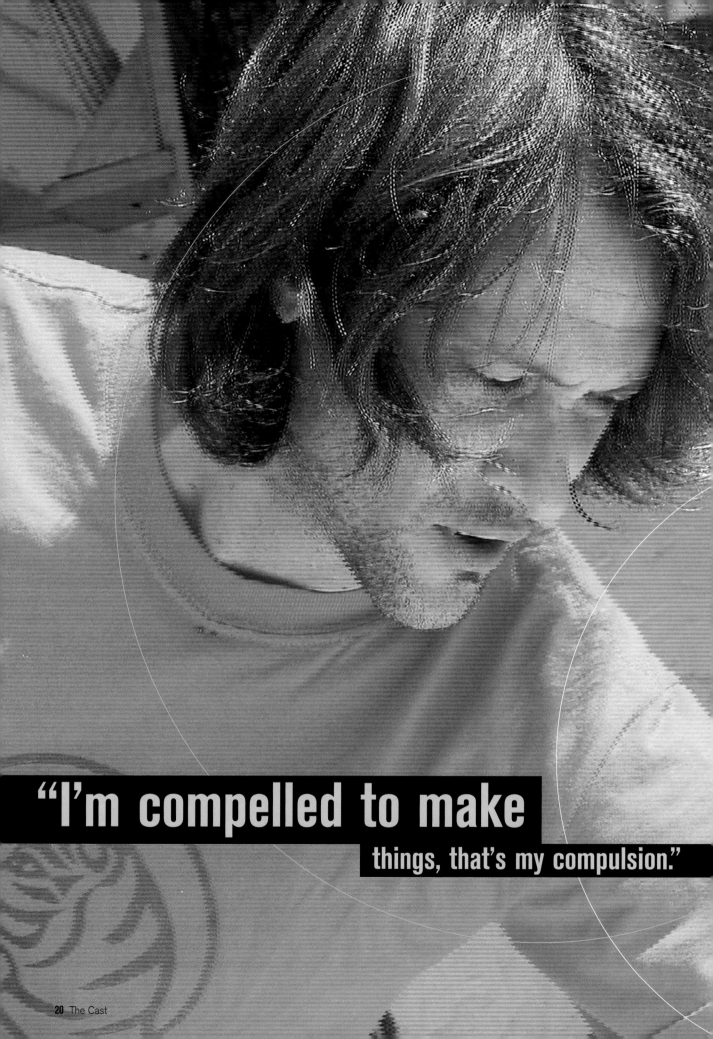

"I'm compelled to make things, that's my compulsion."

# The John Bruce Quiz

**1) When asked what his favorite toy was as a child, did John say:**
**A)** A teddy bear lamp; I redesigned it using sticks when I was 4.
**B)** My first movie camera; I wanted to remake the film *Powers of Ten*.
**C)** Adhesive tape.

**2) When asked how best to begin a room design, did John say:**
**A)** Measure the room and furniture; then draw a floor plan...
**B)** Gather fabric swatches and tear out magazine pages for ideas.
**C)** Start with a mood or a vibe.

**3) When asked what frustrates him, did John say:**
**A)** People who don't know El Greco is Doménikos Theotokópoulos.
**B)** People who feign unconsciousness.
**C)** When the chairs I've requested for a room arrive in the wrong color.

In this tiny space, with production crew members and others buzzing about him, John has less than an hour to implant an image of the room in his mind and check the preliminary plans he made using an amateur video and rough measurements. He leaves with a list of items he and his team will need. Together they spend the afternoon shopping for paint, supplies, and wood, working out design problems in the aisles of a home improvement center.

John is always on the lookout for inspiration. "I start by walking the streets. I bump into things; I peruse bookstores, surf the Internet, keep my eyes open in restaurants, watch old favorite movies and such. I spend a lot of time collecting this raw material and then I start to boil it down—to crystallize the elements into a spread of projects and objects that will fit the job at hand."

He is especially fond of using common materials in new ways, such as when he created a floor lamp from wire mesh normally used to reinforce concrete. He encourages do-it-yourselfers to avoid making assumptions about materials. "Once you categorize and codify it, it can't be anything else," he says. So instead of seeing rolled up wire mesh, he prefers to see a cylindrical object with concentric squares. When studying it further, he finds that lamp parts can be mounted inside the wire

cylinder for a sculptural urban-style floor lamp.

Lighting plays an important role in the spaces that John designs, so he always finds a way to add at least one creative lamp in each makeover. John's design philosophy is based on an old saying of film directors: "Good design is unobtrusive, with the only things really noticed being the lamps." Some of his lighting projects are so innovative that he will spend hours working on a single design.

"I test really ambitious projects at home," John says. Projects such as the back-lit, interactive panels filled with baby oil and colored water, which served as guitar stands, demand some advance engineering, he says, "especially because some unusual materials were needed like very specific rubber molding and a certain type of glass." Despite his prep work John says that there is still a great deal of interpretation and design work that remains when the crew starts taping. "I expect the carpenters to bring [skills] to the table," he says, "and they do, and I am extremely grateful."

As Day One comes to a close, John and his team are still working, now under large spotlights that attract bugs and biting insects. The team knows it has a full day ahead of it so at 9 p. m. John gets his satchel, and they all leave. The evening has cooled now that the sun has set, but for this designer with an innovative vision, the heat is still on.

# Designer Chayse Dacoda

## At 3 she refused to sleep in her bed because the sheets didn't match the comforter. Ever a passionate designer, Chayse Dacoda seeks her signature style.

Chayse Dacoda is hunting the aisles of a home-improvement center the way a cat searches out a mouse. Her tiny form outfitted in safari-inspired activewear, she darts quickly from aisle to aisle.

"There's always a little last-minute shuffling," says Chayse. She's learned to roll with the punches as a 48-hour television designer and is adept at fast solutions. "The hardest part of the show for me is seeing the space only the day before. Often it's hard to get a space's inherent energy and personality through the videotape and photos. It's only by walking into the room that you truly understand the scale and dimensions."

The room in this case is actually a bar in Hilton Head, South Carolina. Chayse dreamed up a dramatic makeover for the space and an inventive system for sending drink orders to the bartender. She discovered a glitch in the system's design after surveying the room in person. Now she and carpenter Andrew Dan-Jumbo are searching for a solution. With only a few hours remaining to gather project materials, they'll have little time to solve the problem before the 48-hour timer begins to tick.

"I would like to experiment with projects at home more," she says. "Sometimes I will try a process of texturing or painting to see if it is going to work as I think it will. But usually there is no time in the prep stage to sit around and play with the idea to see what works."

It's a problem many of the designers have to deal with, and today it's her turn. She has the image of a design in her mind and struggles to translate it into the physical. It will take a couple of pulleys, wire, miscellaneous hardware...and some sort of mechanism.

That's the problem—what is the mechanism that will make it work? Whatever it is, it isn't available. Although it's an interesting design, Chayse has other priorities and decides to scrap the project. Like all of the *While You Were Out* designers, Chayse has to perform spontaneous design magic in a very short time frame, and she's usually successful. On the rare occasion when an idea doesn't work out, it doesn't derail her. She has a lengthy list of other items to gather for the makeover, so without further delay she heads to the paint aisle.

"I like contrast. I like different," she says. White, black, and fuchsia form one of her favorite color palettes, along with "six shades of the same beige with blue and green accents. Each space calls out to me a color scheme, and I like them all." Her designs demonstrate her comfort with color and showcase a style that she describes with words such as "fluid," "elegance," and "contrast."

# The Chayse Dacoda Quiz

**1) When asked how first-time designers should decorate a room, did Chayse say:**

**A)** With a credit card…Better yet, with someone else's credit card.

**B)** Shop at garage sales and flea markets—retro is in and you can find great bargains there.

**C)** With floors and lighting—foundation first, that's my motto.

**2) When asked which three material things she values most, did Chayse say:**

**A)** My autographed photos of Mr. Spock, Captain Kirk, and Dr. McCoy.

**B)** My book of fabric sources, my watch, and my cell phone.

**C)** My bedside lamps—I love them—my laptop, and underwater photos from a diving trip in Thailand.

**3) When asked what advice she has for selecting a wall color, did Chayse say:**

**A)** Paint poster boards in the colors you're considering and audition them.

**B)** Always make the ceiling a lighter shade than the walls.

**C)** There are no rules in design…Have fun with it!

"I like to blend things that contradict," she says, giving examples of items she's combined, such as "linear pieces with ethnic carvings." Her specialty is fusing many elements. "Discovering a room is like looking at a hologram," she explains. "With each layer, you notice more."

Chayse clearly loves the creative, chaotic life of the designer and the experimenting that goes along with it. "I was actually doing interior designing when I was 12 to 14 years old, working for a designer, doing hands-on work, earning a little extra money," she says. "I was always very creative and doing things around the house when I was young."

She tried her hand at several do-it-yourself projects, but when it came time to select a career, she chose one in finance and later turned to real estate; she began styling homes to encourage sales. After she designed her own home, opportunity came knocking. One design job led to another, and finally she won her first whole-house decorating project. The downside was that she had to complete the work in a fraction of the time most designers demand, but her can-do attitude persuaded her to take the job.

"I had 45 days to pull together a five-bedroom house for a man with three children. I assembled a team of builders and painters and electricians and found every piece of furniture. He and the kids moved in, very happy, on day 46," Chayse recalls. Later she was selected to be one of the pioneering designers for *While You Were Out.*

Chayse and the others finish their shopping in the home-improvement center, then load the truck. The day is going by quickly, and they still have three stores to visit before closing time. At this point it's pure determination that gets Chayse through traffic on unfamiliar roads, and she manages to obtain the necessary sheets of glass, custom-size stone, and fabric store items.

It's Chayse's love of design that encourages her to press on, even when things occasionally go awry. She is serious about her work, yet she also knows how to relax. "I can be totally off-the-wall," she says—but not today. Right now she needs to keep her mind on the task so another happy ending can be realized. "There are a million things to be thinking about," she says. "It's up to the will of the designer if things are going to get done." Luckily for the *While You Were Out* homeowners, that's a lesson this passionate designer learned early, at the age of 3.

**"I really try to zone in** to the homeowner's personality and energy level."

# Designer Nadia Geller

## Determined to create fresh and exciting rooms, Nadia Geller uses vibrant color and vintage finds to pump new life into boring spaces.

free expression comes naturally to Nadia Geller, a self-described quirky New York designer, with a penchant for global and retro looks. "I was a vintage-store junkie from a young age," Nadia says. "My hair has been every color in the rainbow."

On this day, for a show in Jacksonville, Florida, Nadia's hair is a conservative reddish brown, and she's twisted it under a scarf for a streetwise 'do. She's dressed in sleek black pants with silver-zippered pockets and a colorful, artsy blouse. She has a style all her own, and it changes with her mood. This chic biker-meets-urban-artist look communicates her present frame of mind.

The interiors that Nadia designs are gutsy. They feature a fearless use of strong graphic shapes and big-drama colors, such as fuchsia with red, or purple with copper. Loud nostalgia colors, such as turquoise and flamingo pink, have also found their way into her design plans.

"My rooms always have a vibrant and colorful feeling," says Nadia. "I love color schemes that remind me of nature and the outdoors. My favorite one right now reminds me of the Grand Canyon: warm rusty oranges, reds, and hints of a crisp sky blue."

Nadia's preference for drama is also present in her furniture selections, which are often a conglomeration of old and new, quirky and sensible—all with something to say.

"My style is a combination of contemporary twisted with special and unique features," she says. "The rooms I design are more of a collection and collaboration of new and old pieces of furniture, with hints of color and texture that bring the room together."

Furniture budgets on the show are limited, so for the most part Nadia either recycles or has pieces built by the carpenters. When she does buy, she is apt to mix anything from ethnic to contemporary, from Bohemian to Danish Modern, giving her rooms a multicultural, global look.

"I like my rooms to have their own personalities that make their inhabitants comfortable and excited to be in the space," says Nadia. "I also feel that it is important to use pieces, furniture or accessories, that have personal meaning to the owner." All these elements create an appealing mix, giving Nadia's rooms a comfortable, lived-in look.

As a former retail-display designer for a New York design store, Nadia learned about furniture and accessory trends, and she still keeps her finger on the pulse. When she is working on a room design, she often goes for walks through retail

"I get bored having the rooms in my home the same way for more than a year."

# The Nadia Geller Quiz

**1) When asked what she thought of her newest hair color, did Nadia say:**

A) I can't wait to color it again…Next time I'm going with primary-color stripes!

B) Lucy is my hero. When I saw this color I thought it would honor her but not be too bold for my skin color.

C) I look a lot like my mom and it kind of freaked me out.

**2) When asked which college sport she participated in, did Nadia say:**

A) I was a B-ball player with street moves…Watch out, I'm fast.

B) I came from an athletic family…I was a runner in college.

C) The only sport I was involved in was art.

**3) When asked what jobs she's had while living in New York, did Nadia say:**

A) I was a hair colorist at one of the finest pet salons.

B) I waitressed for a very long time…I was a nanny…I was a TV studio manager.

C) I sold Harley-Davidsons to inside traders on Wall Street.

stores or visits bars, restaurants, and home-furnishing stores for ideas. "I continue to be influenced by movies, theater, different cultures, and amazing furniture and home-accessory designers who combine form with function," she says.

Today Nadia is working frantically to put into play a design plan she worked out a few weeks ago. It's an unusual assignment: transforming a football stadium conference room. The space is commercial, but she approaches it in the same way as a residential space.

"I start out with the furniture that is in the room," she says. "I like to take a day to think about what I want to create and then sketch it out. Then I make a floor plan and elevations of each area." The floor plan and her beautifully drawn elevations help the rest of the *While You Were Out* team understand what she hopes to accomplish. Nadia also tries to identify potential problems before starting the room.

"As the designer it is my job to make sure that enough money is budgeted for each project." She designs her projects and purchases some of the materials for the show in advance. The team hunts down other items locally. "For the most part there is collaboration between the seamstresses and the carpenters for the best materials and methods," she says.

"I have a very detailed and thought-out design for each show, and it is my job to see that my final design is made. The more organized and detailed for the crew, the better my design will be," says Nadia.

But even the best-laid plans sometimes go awry, a fact she realizes when installing the room: The newly applied cork on the walls is too dull, and there isn't enough fabric to slipcover all of the chairs.

"Since *While You Were Out* is a reality design show, I don't make any prototypes for the episodes. I like to challenge myself by doing new things for the camera without knowing the result." But knowing that she is backed by experienced carpenters and other creative people gives her confidence. "Everyone who works on the show is so talented," says Nadia.

She considers the problems this makeover is presenting. She reviews her options, takes an inventory of yet unused fabric with carpenter Leslie Segrete, and thinks about how the changes she's planning will impact her overall design.

After a few minutes, she decides to spray-paint the cork for more visual power and asks Leslie to design the two slipcovers to incorporate remnants from the window treatment—bold moves from a fearless leader. Nadia scores big on the final play!

# Designer Mark Montano

## He's a happy soul with a desire to create. Mark Montano shows the world of serious design how to have a lot more fun.

Mark Montano's room designs can be described in one word: happy. This descriptor is not commonly used for interiors, but in Mark's case it's appropriate. "My designs have to have a sense of humor," says Mark, explaining that he prefers a relaxed style with an uplifting spirit. "I don't like stuffy design at all. I don't like to take spaces too seriously."

Often his rooms are colorful and energized spaces with the goal of making the people who live and visit there feel good. "A psychologist friend told me once that she knew she would like me as soon as she saw my apartment—that it was a direct reflection of who I am as a person. When I looked around, she was right. I surround myself with things I love; I experiment; I use color and always have a bit of humor somewhere," says Mark.

His current home, an apartment in New York City's trendy East Village, is colorful and eclectic. The office/living area is African-inspired, with masks, maps, and cabinets holding his personal treasures. His kitchen has its own personality, featuring brightly colored, harlequin-pattern walls and polka-dot dishes. And the bedroom is an over-the-top design

that Mark loves. "It's French with glass lamps and brocade bedding," he says. It's clearly a space that feeds his designer soul and brings him joy. "Most people love my apartment," he says.

His desire to create comes naturally. His mother is an artist, and as a child he often would strive to be creative like her. "I grew up in a small town, La Junta, Colorado. I have five younger brothers, and that was really, really fun. There weren't a lot of resources. If you wanted something really cool, you pretty much had to make it," he says. This environment fed his talent, and by his early teens, Mark was making a lot of things, including clothing for his mother.

When it came time for college, Mark took a traditional route and got a degree in business from Colorado State University. That choice helped him learn needed skills, but those skills never pushed aside his first love. "I am not really sure if I have a head for business. My main concern all of my life was how to live comfortably and be able to get up in the morning and create something every day—either paint or sew, draw or write," he says with a laugh.

Mark comes from a long line of creative people, and from them he has learned the skills he uses today. "My mother writes poetry and draws," he says. "My aunts used to

# The Mark Montano Quiz

**1) When asked what his favorite gift was as a child, did Mark say:**

A) A walking, talking robot with purple eyes.

B) Art supplies—sketch pads, pencils, crayons, markers, and pens.

C) A building set—I was into design even as a kid.

**2) When asked how his bedroom is decorated, did Mark say:**

A) It's very tailored and neutral, like a classic suit that is comfortable and never goes out of style.

B) It's the one room that hasn't been decorated. I'll do it when I have time.

C) There's a birdcage theme and a fantastically ornate chandelier hanging above the bed.

**3) When asked where his design inspiration comes from, did Mark say:**

A) I'm not influenced by anything or anyone—only my ever-morphing mind.

B) Old movies—maybe that's why I like black and white color palettes!

C) My mother's art. I like to surround myself with her paintings.

let me help them sew when I was very young, so I know my way around a sewing machine. My grandfather and uncles were all carpenters and sculptors, so I was also trained there." Understanding the techniques behind so many creative outlets has greatly empowered him. "I think that if I can imagine it, then I know there is a way for it to be done," Mark says.

After Colorado State, Mark attended New York City's Fashion Institute of Technology, where he earned a master's degree in costume history. He interned at Oscar de la Renta, where he gained an appreciation for exquisite fabrics and the inspiration to begin his own fashion line. Since then he's melded the worlds of fashion, publishing, decorating, and now television.

"Fashion and interiors are very similar. They are shape, balance, form, and function," he says. "I love designing rooms for *While You Were Out*, because people are willing to experiment and try new things. It would be boring to do the same old room over and over, just like it would be boring to wear the same dress over and over."

So how does Mark Montano go about designing a room for a *While You Were Out* homeowner? "What I try to do is learn what they need in this room. Then I go from there. I always advise getting rid of things and starting with a clean space. Next I pick the color scheme and stick to it no matter what. After that, we start adding until it feels right." His personal all-time favorite color scheme is black, white, and red. His favorite fabric is light green silk Jacquard with golden yellow accents. But these choices seldom show up in his designs for other people. "I try to pick colors that will look good on them physically. For example, I have olive skin, so I painted my bathroom olive green. I'm surrounded by a color that makes me look good," he explains.

As for the rest of the process, Mark says, "I approach it creatively. I dress a room. I'm figuring out the best way to make it the most exciting environment possible." Of designs that don't quite add up, he says, "If it doesn't always work out the way I plan it, that's part of the fun of the show. I can't tell you how many projects have found their way into the garbage."

But finding new, successful projects isn't a problem for Mark. While absorbing loads of sensory input from the outside world, he looks within for inspiration and generates endless ideas. The colorful, wonderful spaces he designs often have only one thing in common: They're as delightful and fun as Mark himself.

**"I am constantly inspired** by the world around me, and I can't seem to shut it off."

# Carpenter Ali Barone

## From stilettos to sergers, pearls to plywood, Ali Barone is a can-do woman who is ready to tackle projects with a smile. And she does them all without breaking a nail.

**a**li Barone enters the backyard patio and joins the design team as it prepares to set up *Carpentry World*. It is a typical Day One on a *While You Were Out* set, as the cameras start rolling to capture the early scenes of the show—the unloading of the familiar trailer that carries saws, rolling carts filled with tools, worktables, sewing machines, and everything else a two-day makeover requires.

The cast and crew are dressed much alike. Everyone wears khakis or aged jeans, relaxed T-shirts in white or grayed-down colors, and comfortable work boots or shoes—that is, everyone but Ali. She wears a lipstick pink, form-fitting sleeveless top with dark slacks, and her long hair has been curled becomingly. She has placed a matching pink flower in her hair above her ear. "Most people who I meet in New York City are always a bit taken aback by my appearance," she says. "I'm a lot taller in my heels, which I prefer over work boots in my off time."

She's pretty in pink and has even worn June Cleaver pearl earrings and a matching necklace on occasion. However, she is anything but pampered. "My list is very extensive on every show," she says. "On any given episode I usually sew four to eight pillows, two to four sets of curtains; custom-build a few accent pieces for the room, like end tables and shelves; and execute several crafty 'makey-do' projects." And that's in addition to unloading the truck, helping set up *Carpentry World* and other workstations, and assisting with the room installation.

Ali was born in Brooklyn, but her New Yorker parents wanted her and her older brother to experience the great outdoors and a more "rustic" life. With that goal in mind, the family moved out of the city congestion and built a log cabin at the end of a dirt road that overlooked a forest and mountains.

As she grew up, Ali would often hang out with her brother and his friends. "We knew the woods, berries, and what leaves were what," she says. But she also liked playing with fashion dolls, styling hair, and using her stapler-style, hand-sewing machine to design clothing. "I'm very comfortable with both the masculine and feminine sides of my personality," she explains. The skills that she learned, along with her education (including a BFA in set design and a master's degree in elementary education), prepared her for her multilayered position as a *While You Were Out* carpenter.

"I love collaborating and creating with everyone. It's a great feeling to put time and effort into something that is going to bring someone so much joy," says Ali. She

"Our show loves to present new challenges and watch us rise to the occasion, so…the sky's the limit!"

# The Ali Barone Quiz

**1) When asked what her greatest challenge was growing up, did Ali say:**

**A) Keeping up with the boys—I could build that tree house too.**

**B) Baking pies, but cooking is not my strong suit.**

**C) Learning to wear high heels while carrying lumber.**

**2) When asked what type of pet she has, did Ali say:**

**A) A bulldog named Petunia.**

**B) A parakeet named Killer.**

**C) A rabbit named Pinky Tuscadero.**

**3) When asked how she would decorate her bedroom, did Ali say:**

**A) With exotic, romantic fabrics, furniture, and art that I personally collect.**

**B) With a granny quilt—I have used silk, satin, velvet, tapestry, and even parts of my wedding dress.**

**C) With a bed I built myself and bedding I sewed.**

learned the importance of teamwork as a scenic artist and designer, working a grueling schedule to create sets for shows such as *Beauty and the Beast*, TV's *Pulp Comics*, and various commercials. During this time she also learned how to stretch a design dollar.

"I find my best bargains on the street! I confess I am a garbage picker. I love to refinish eclectic finds, whether it's painting, staining, or reupholstering." She has scouted many shops and stores that are not typical designer haunts, where she finds furniture, accessories, and project materials. "I also go to consignment shops in search of a good bargain. And dollar stores can produce some interesting items, believe it or not."

"We often use a variety of materials in new and exciting ways that are somewhat experimental," Ali continues. "It's part of the challenge and it can create a true sense of jeopardy." Using unusual or unexpected materials in new ways is something she's required to do, especially with some of the innovative designs that are, at times, part of a *While You Were Out* interior.

On a recent show, designer John Bruce asked Ali to use a very stiff, industrial-strength synthetic fabric to create a woven bedspread. "It was, in my opinion, the antithesis of what most people would choose to adorn their bed," says Ali, who nevertheless carried out the

designer's wishes. Now, she admits, "I have to say, when it was completed, it looked clean and simple, while adding a textural element that worked extremely well with the theme of the room."

Ali gets her yard goods in New York shops known for bargains. "I have a few fabric stores that I like on Broadway in SoHo for really beautiful Italian silks, for $15 and under a yard. There is a great trim store over there too," she says. For paint, Ali checks home improvement centers for bargains. "I often go to the 'oops' paint section and try to color-match."

As for her ideas on room designing, Ali says, "I think if you pick a theme or a color palette and stick to it without the pressure that everything has to match perfectly, but rather simply tie together, you can easily create very comfortable and interesting rooms." She says that "elements that unify the room" and "objects displayed in artful compositions" are also key to a good design.

Ali's personal preference is rooms with warmth. "I'm very stimulated by color. I will never be a person with all white walls or all white furniture—I want warmth," she says. Her favorite color palette is autumnal golds, oranges, reds, russets, and browns. "I had the most spectacular falls growing up in a cozy, comfortable cabin surrounded by trees that would be a blaze of beautiful colors," she says. "I always found it the most inspiring time of year."

Answer Key: 1) A 2) A 3) A

# Carpenter
# Jason
# Cameron

## He's the quiet craftsman with a heart as big as his biceps. Jason Cameron's two favorite things in life—carpentry and being in front of the camera—come together.

Jason Cameron is living his dream. "I get paid to do what I love to do and I get to do it on TV—it's awesome!" Jason says. Born in Toledo, Ohio, and raised in Marquette, Michigan, Jason is the son of an electrician father and a very determined mother. Jason's father did roofing and construction on the side, and Jason learned the basics of the trades at a tender age. "I can't remember the first thing I built," he says. His mother is his true inspiration, though. "My father left when I was 10. It was my mother, my two brothers, and me," he explains. "I decided right then and there that I would become the man of the house and help my mom with anything that needed to be done. Everything I am today, I owe to my mother. She raised three boys on her own with nothing more than a high school education. She not only encouraged me verbally to pursue my dreams, but more importantly, she inspired me through her actions." To support her family, Jason's mother did nontraditional jobs. She also put herself through college, graduating with honors. She was recently named "Teacher of the Year."

With his mother's spirit of determination, Jason pursued his own dreams, using carpentry as a cushion. While attending Northern Michigan University, he relied on part-time carpentry jobs for income and tuition. In 1999 Jason headed to New York City to pursue a career in modeling and acting. Although he got regular work as a model and actor, he still fell back on carpentry to make ends meet between jobs. That's how he ended up on *While You Were Out.*

"I was remodeling a condo when my agent called and asked me to go to a casting for a television show ASAP. I had no time to change or clean up. I went as I was, covered in drywall dust, dirty, and wearing my tool belt," says Jason. "After the casting, the casting director pulled me aside and told me that she thought I would be perfect for another show she was casting. She asked if I'd ever seen *While You Were Out.* I told her I watched it all the time. She arranged for a meeting that day. So I guess it was kind of fitting that I was wearing my tool belt, because a month later I was signing the contract!"

He's now a TV carpenter and regularly on the road, but Jason hasn't let that buff model body fall by the wayside. A certified personal trainer, he's still diligent about his twice-daily workouts—cardio in the morning and a full workout in the afternoon. A plastic box of vitamins and a healthy breakfast (usually oatmeal) are his mainstay, along with time in the gym. "When I travel, the first thing I ask at the hotel is, 'Where is the gym?'" he says. If there's no gym, he improvises by lifting furniture instead of

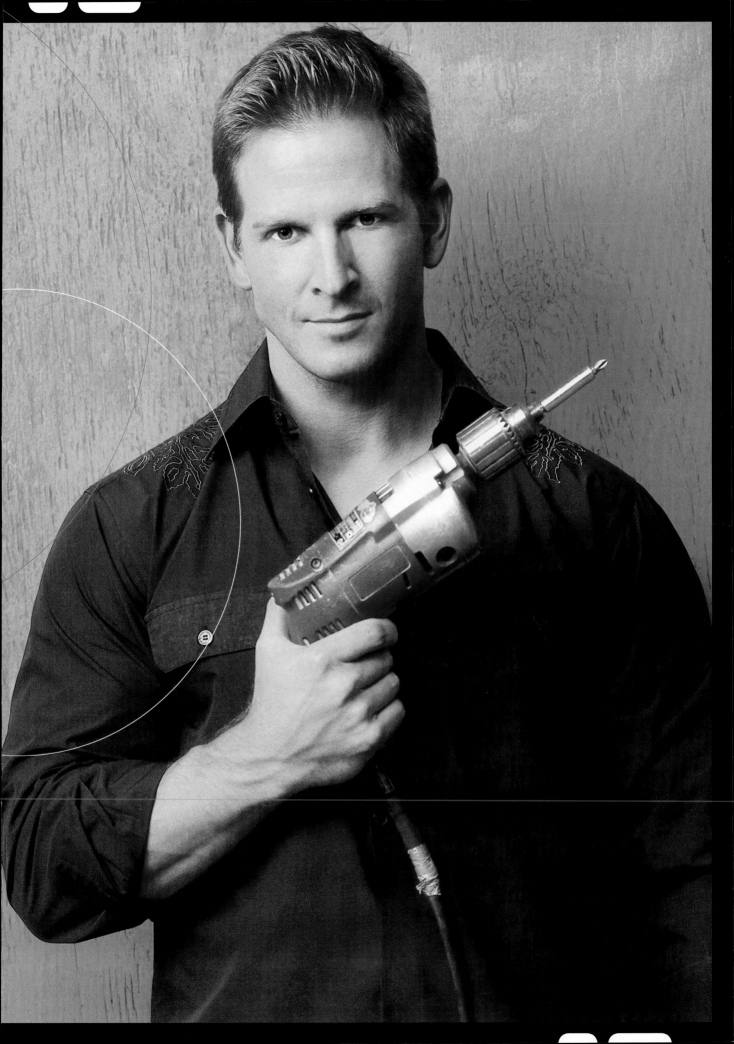

# The Jason Cameron Quiz

**1) When asked to name the best gift he ever received, did Jason say:**

**A)** Cowboy boots, because they make me look tall and lean.

**B)** A camera so I can keep a scrapbook of all my projects.

**C)** My wife.

**2) When asked what he is best skilled at, did Jason say:**

**A)** Building extremely heavy pieces. Just ask Evan, since he usually gets stuck carrying them with me.

**B)** Pumping iron.

**C)** Unloading the truck—I can do it by myself in less than 5 minutes.

**3) When asked what would be his dream project for WYWO, did Jason say:**

**A)** A kitchen with lots of granite countertops and a big commercial stove.

**B)** A home gym with all the newest equipment and plenty of weights.

**C)** A really cool tree house.

weights, both in the hotel and on the set.

Evan Farmer knows Jason and his routines well. "Jason is probably the most disciplined person I've ever met," says Evan. "Look at his body, for crying out loud! He's extremely organized. He's the guy you know will come in and do a task on time and do it to a T. He's the essence of reliability."

That discipline makes for efficiency when building major components of a room under a nearly impossible deadline. "On a show like this, it is a must that I have a good project priority list and cut list [wood pieces in the dimensions needed]. The more prepared I am going in, the more time I save. I usually write up my cut list the night before Day Zero [shopping day]. I have a cut list for each project I make. A good cut list not only saves me time, but it also gives me a more accurate materials list. This is important because I have a very tight budget for lumber and I can't waste money on a lot of scrap," explains Jason.

Keeping his tools organized is another one of Jason's keys to success. "All of the tools I use are kept on the truck. Each carpenter is responsible for their own set of tools, but we share the power tools and the two large bins that contain a wide range of specialty tools and bits," he says.

A couple of hours before the

reveal, most of the tools and equipment are organized, put away, and loaded onto the truck. "We keep out only the tools we need to finish what we're still working on. The prop masters not only drive the truck all over the country, but they do an amazing job at keeping it stocked and organized. I'd be lost without them," Jason says.

Like everyone else on the show, Jason strives to do a good job. "As far as I know, all the projects I've made on the show thus far have been well received by the homeowners. I take pride in everything I build and want nothing more than the homeowners to be happy with what I build. That's important to me," he says.

On the surface, Jason may look like he's all business and brawn, but deep down he's also a lot of heart. "I love my family and care about people. Even as a kid, I was the person who cared if people felt good about themselves when other kids were into picking on each other," he says. "My real goal now is to be successful, raise a family, and be a good father. I take care of my responsibilities because I don't worry about things when I can control them. I think I have a pretty good balance. I work long hours, but I always make time for myself and my family. I work hard, but when I'm not working, I play hard."

# "This show requires
## a serious team effort!"

# Carpenter Andrew Dan-Jumbo

## A man of words, with the shirts to prove it, Andrew Dan-Jumbo is a talented carpenter and a free-spirited, rugged individualist with something to say.

a ndrew Dan-Jumbo wears lettered T-shirts the way a newspaper wears a headline. Some state the obvious, others tell of his mood, quirky humor, or an opinion. He started wearing the shirts in the first season, when a *While You Were Out* soundman gave him one that said, "Everyone's entitled to my opinion." From then on Andrew started collecting T-shirts with all types of expressions.

"I have a massive amount of T-shirts, at least 300," he says. Over the years he has found it's easiest to store them in a trunk on the *While You Were Out* trailer, so just the right one is handy when he needs it. "I wear them two or three times, then I retire them," says Andrew. The words and phrases are diverse. Some of the irreverent ones include "Your Girlfriend Thinks I'm Hot" and "Dork," which pairs nicely with fellow carpenter Leslie Segrete's "Dorks are Hot" T-shirt.

Other shirts carry messages intended for the *While You Were Out* designers. These include "It's not my problem," "I'm retired," "No really, let me drop everything so I can take care of your problem," and the ever popular "Employee of the Month."

Since being hired as the first carpenter on *While You Were Out*, Andrew Dan-Jumbo has become one of home-improvement television's most recognized faces. He was included in *People* magazine's "50 Most Beautiful People" (May 2003) and he has been on talk shows and magazine spreads. While Andrew is popular with fans, he strives for carpentry perfection under extreme time restrictions.

"I have had little formal training in carpentry; for the most part I am self-taught," Andrew says. "As a child I was always encouraged to explore and investigate the mechanics of everyday items, to get a sense of how they work and why they are made a certain way. This helped me develop good motor skills and has made it easy for me to pick up trades like carpentry because they rely on good hand-eye coordination and an understanding of engineering," he explains.

His enterprising nature and strong work ethic reflect his parents' influence. His mother and father were torn apart during Nigeria's civil war. His father, a surgeon, stayed in Nigeria, and his mother took the children to a safe place, Shoreham, a coastal town near London, England. Andrew grew up there and eventually attended London's St. Martin's College of Art and Design, although his father's wish was that Andrew would follow in his footsteps. "I was his last kid and he hoped I would become a doctor," Andrew says. But Andrew found his sister's art college classes more to his

# "A well-designed room

### has to balance form with function."

# The Andrew Dan-Jumbo Quiz

**1) When asked whether he has a favorite tool, did Andrew say:**

**A)** My tool belt with my hammer, screwdriver, tape measure, and pliers.

**B)** I have no favorites. I love them all equally.

**C)** Yes, my brain!

**2) When asked what emergency items he uses for carpentry success, did Andrew say:**

**A)** Extra wood so I can cut twice if I only measure once.

**B)** Duct tape!

**C)** For bad weather I have rain gear and a good tent.

**3) When asked what is the most unusual thing he's built, did Andrew say:**

**A)** John Bruce's kaleidoscope table in Episode 251, *John Bruce—Untitled.*

**B)** A bridge that connected the mainland to an island—we had to drain the lake.

**C)** An all-wood reclining chair that we painted purple.

liking and became a graphic designer and commercial artist instead.

Andrew says his parents are well-read and taught him to love language and knowledge. "They impressed upon us the importance of being well-spoken and articulate," he adds. During their formative years, Andrew says, he and his siblings were raised "in the company of people with very high standards who chose their words carefully."

Andrew emphasizes that the best gift he ever got was encouragement from his mom. "Despite all she had to do, she dragged me to history, science, art museums, protest marches to save the whales, etcetera. This led me to be inquisitive—to wonder why certain things are a certain way," he says. She also encouraged him to "strive to figure things out" for himself.

He and his brother used these problem-solving skills to their advantage and launched a commercial and residential construction company that specializes in historic restorations and new home developments in Buffalo, New York. This business led to Andrew's being discovered by *While You Were Out.*

Andrew credits his diverse background with preparing him to handle the requirements of the job. "I tap into my years of construction experience and I always build a project first in my head, anticipating potential problems before they arise," he says. "My background in art has been invaluable in the development of the design aesthetic [for] the pieces that I build. The plans I am given vary in detail depending on the designer and the time that the designer has had to develop his or her ideas. I am usually relied on to take the basic piece and develop it to produce a finished product that most complements the design goal," he explains. "I actually enjoy the challenge of resolving the many budget and construction challenges in the short time frames that we operate under. It's exciting!"

Although he doesn't always get to use his first-choice materials, Andrew tries to ensure that all projects are well-crafted. He's been forced to come to terms with fabricating in a rush and the mistakes that occur in the midst of the chaos. "It's awesome to have the opportunity to showcase my skills on national TV, although of course my mistakes also air nationally," he admits. "That's reality TV, I suppose." When he can, Andrew enjoys creating projects that require furniture-grade craftmanship.

"I believe in 'patience is a virtue,' for only if you pay close attention to the job at hand can you achieve a truly high standard of fit and finish, which is always my number one goal," he says. "I really try hard to maintain a high standard of build quality and create pieces the homeowners can enjoy for years to come. It's always wise to remember that we are not only filming a show in their homes, but that we are their guests, invited in as professionals and trusted to produce pieces that best reflect our show."

# Carpenter Leslie Segrete

## Leslie Segrete jokes that if she were on *Gilligan's Island,* she'd be "the plain girl, Mary Ann." But this Jill-of-all-trades could just as well be the brainy professor.

Sewing slipcovers is second nature to Leslie Segrete, a self-taught seamstress who tackles complex design projects fearlessly on-camera for *While You Were Out*. Trained as a scenic designer, she possesses a resume that includes big-name projects for which she honed a myriad of hands-on design skills: sewing, carpentry, and fabricating all sorts of oddball items, including golden plungers and stuffed pigeons.

When she was hired by *While You Were Out* to work in front of the camera, it took some getting used to, even for this spunky New York native with notable abilities and a knack for physical comedy. "For me this whole life is like a dream," says Leslie. "I have always worked in this area, but never in front of the camera. It feels funny to get so much attention." But this is no glamour job. Designing and sewing slipcovers, skillfully fashioned to hide a plethora of upholstery sins, isn't easy—especially with a limited amount of time and fabric.

"When you design sets for many plays and the school only has a few pieces of furniture to use on the sets, you quickly figure out how to make an apple look less like an apple, and then eventually you get better and that apple becomes an orange," she says.

craftspeople. When we all put our heads together, crazy things can happen," says Leslie. Her confident and relaxed approach quickly decreases the situational stress. Leslie has good reason to feel relaxed: designing is in her genes. "I learned about building from my dreamer and architect father. He was always making or designing something, so I came to understand the inside workings of how things are made," says Leslie.

Although she inherited her father's heart and mind for design, Leslie didn't get his professional New York office. Instead, she works in makeshift spaces—a corner of a homeowner's garage or in a cracker-box bedroom—setting up her bountiful supply cart along with folding tables, sewing machines, and the like.

"That is my office, essentially," she says, and keeping order is important. "I always

Today this queen of carpentry and cover-ups will be put to the test. She must design a slew of slipcovers—more than a dozen, without a pattern—to cover dowdy office chairs in a conference room at the Jacksonville Jaguar stadium. Unfortunately for her, fabric is in short supply and window coverings are also on the "to do" list. She is also scheduled to help paint the room and build carpentry projects.

"Thankfully, I work with many skilled

# The Leslie Segrete Quiz

**1) When asked which tool she couldn't live without, did Leslie say:**

A) My sewing machine; without it I'd be using a needle and thread.

B) My glue gun, because it helps with sticky design problems.

C) Definitely a staple gun; this handy tool will get you out of almost any jam.

**2) When asked about her personal design style, did Leslie say:**

A) I try to collect pieces that would make it seem like Indiana Jones lives here. If I had my way, I'd name my firstborn child Indiana Jones!

B) I collect stuff from the Monkees—I'd like to name my firstborn Davy Jones!

C) I collect music CDs…If I had my way, I'd name my firstborn child Tom Jones!

**3) When asked how many turkeys she made in a two-week period for a morning show, did Leslie say:**

A) 47 turkeys for celebrity chefs—by Thanksgiving I could carve one in three minutes.

B) 22 turkeys for football players—after that I decided they were the turkeys.

C) 2 turkeys—I found out after the show they were still frozen on the inside.

---

make sure that I know what I am running low on, and what is good to have on hand in the event of an emergency. I always organize my bins and work area first thing, Day One, to double-check that I have what I need, and then I keep things neat as I go, so no supplies are left behind or accidentally tossed."

Logistics is always a concern, even in the best filming locations, because Leslie generally has only a few hours to complete a week's worth of assignments. For this show she'll get no home field advantage: Her "office" will be in the opposing team's locker room a football-field-width away from the conference room.

It's chilly, and Leslie walks quickly across the windswept field. Her long dark hair whips uncontrollably about her head and slaps at her cheeks. She makes a silly face and captures the unruly mass in her hands.

Inside the locker room, she is all business. She holds the fabric up to the chairs to determine how to place the stripes. Then she considers options with designer Nadia Geller in case she has to improvise for a fabric shortage.

"Slipcovers are tricky," she says later. For sofas and love seats, she suggests studying each part as a separate area and taking a lot of measurements. "I always

treat the seat cushions as their own entity; they get their own covers. This allows the slipcover to stay in place when the item is being used," she says.

For most of the sewing projects, Leslie uses basic supplies. "You really don't need more than a basic sewing machine, nothing fancy-pants," she says. "A pin magnet will make you happier than you could have ever imagined." As for other tools, her must-haves include a 120-inch tape measure, for making draperies; dressmaker's chalk, or some type of marking device; thread—white and a dark neutral; and sharp scissors ("For fabric use only—no Christmas paper!" she warns).

After measuring, cutting, and sewing, Leslie is ready to create her last two slipcovers—but there is not enough fabric. Designer Nadia Geller asks her to use remnants from the window fabric. Leslie assumes an almost professorial stance as she assesses how much fabric she'll need for the slipcovers, scratches her head, and thinks. After a quick calculation, she has the answer: She'll inset the leftover contrasting fabric down the center of each remaining slipcover and place the chairs at opposite ends of the table. Far from plain, it's a winning solution that's definitely brainy.

## "Stop being afraid!
First learn to thread your machine and then learn a straight stitch; the other stitches come later."

Ali

Leslie

Jason

Andrew

John

Chayse

Mark

Nadia

Evan

# The
# rooms

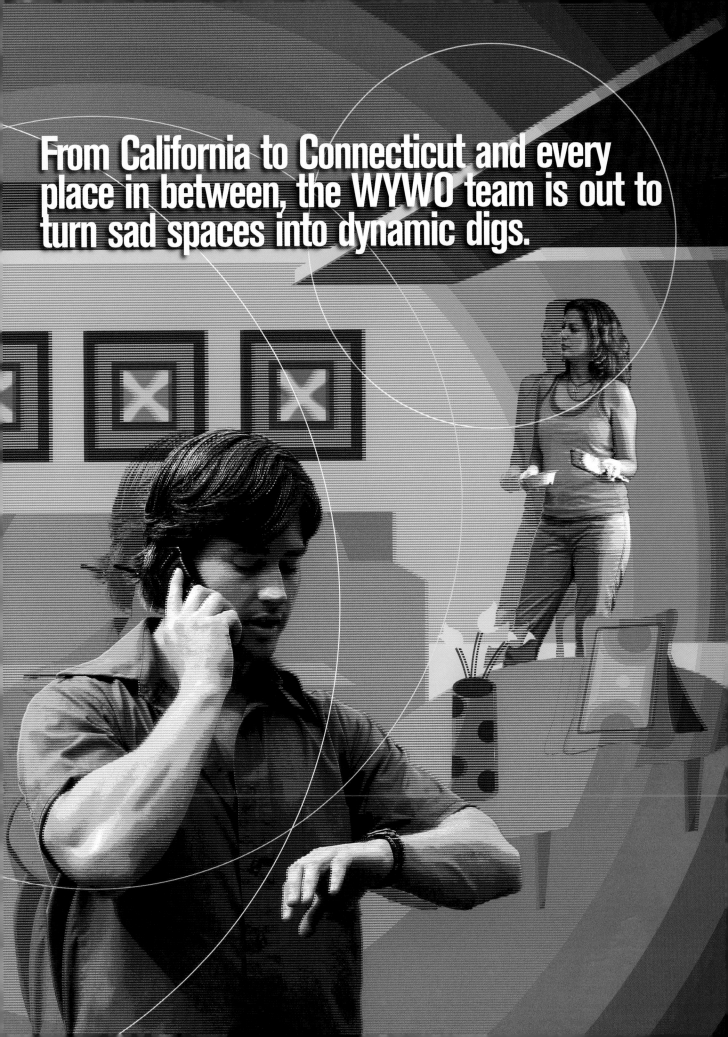

From California to Connecticut and every place in between, the WYWO team is out to turn sad spaces into dynamic digs.

**Living the Dream**: Episode 248, Palm Tree Paradise, Middleburg, Florida. Host: Evan Farmer. Designer: Nadia Geller. Carpenters: Jason Cameron and Leslie Segrete. Episode 251, John Bruce-Untitled, Savannah, Georgia. Host: Evan Farmer. Designer: John Bruce. Carpenters: Leslie Segrete and Andrew Dan-Jumbo. Episode 253, Comfortable Caravan, Williamsburg, Virginia. Host: Evan Farmer. Designer: Mark Montano. Carpenters: Ali Barone and Andrew Dan-Jumbo. Episode 246, 'Take Eames, Fire!' St. Augustine, Florida. Host: Evan Farmer. Designer: John Bruce. Carpenters: Jason Cameron and Ali Barone. **Suite Dreams**: Episode 242, Midnight Cowgirl, Austin, Texas. Host: Evan Farmer. Designer: Chayse Dacoda. Carpenters: Ali Barone and Jason Cameron. Episode 244, Birmingham Imaginarium, Birmingham, Alabama. Host: Evan Farmer. Designer: Mark Montano. Carpenters: Leslie Segrete and Andrew Dan-Jumbo. Episode 256, The Southern Suite, Lexington, Kentucky. Host: Evan Farmer. Designer: Chayse Dacoda. Carpenters: Andrew Dan-Jumbo and Ali Barone. **Big Dreams**: Episode 260, Miracle Myles and the Big Beautiful Basement, Nashville, Tennessee. Host: Evan Farmer. Designer: John Bruce. Carpenters: Andrew Dan-Jumbo and Leslie Segrete. Episode 241, Shades of Water, Austin, Texas. Host: Evan Farmer. Designer: Chayse Dacoda. Carpenters: Ali Barone and Jason Cameron. Episode 259, Cloud Nine Kitchen, Nashville, Tennessee. Host: Evan Farmer. Designer: John Bruce. Carpenters: Andrew Dan-Jumbo and Leslie Segrete. **Day Dreams**: Episode 252, Montano's Mystery, Richmond, Virginia. Host: Evan Farmer. Designer: Mark Montano. Carpenters: Leslie Segrete and Andrew Dan-Jumbo. Episode 258, Global Rhythm Garage, Nashville, Tennessee. Host: Evan Farmer. Designer: Mark Montano. Carpenters: Andrew Dan-Jumbo and Leslie Segrete. Episode 245, Sweet Disco Alabama, Birmingham, Alabama. Host: Evan Farmer. Designer: Nadia Geller. Carpenters: Leslie Segrete and Andrew Dan-Jumbo.

# Living the
## Dream

**The WYWO team brings the good times home, by adding color and theme decorating to family and living rooms.**

# Palm Tree Paradise

## Jack's trailer house rocks with a 1950s vibe after Nadia Geller, the WYWO team, and Jack's roommate, Arwen, turn his drab television room into a relaxing paradise.

**a**rwen and Jack, now 25, have been best friends since junior high school. They share a mobile home in an off-the-beaten-track area of Middleburg, Florida. According to Arwen, Jack is a creative guy and has tried to decorate their outdated, fake-wood-paneled living room the best he could, using beach finds and furniture he built. Arwen says Jack is a "champion" for those in need, and she wants this dream makeover to reward her generous friend.

"I want to do this for Jack, for being such a supportive friend for so many years," says Arwen. To get Jack out of the house, she and the folks at *While You Were Out* cooked up a bogus Florida tourism-board trip for him and his cousin, Sarah. When the coast was clear, designer Nadia Geller, host Evan Farmer, and carpenters Jason Cameron and Leslie Segrete converged on the site to install the room.

### Plan the Design

Nadia uses a three-ring binder to keep her plans, costs, elevation drawings, and swatches organized while she works on the project. In the binder she includes a detailed floor plan that she made after carefully evaluating the physical features of the room and

The 1950s tourist-kitsch design features a dramatic palm tree floor lamp, a prize. Jack's wing chair wears a new slipcover. Nearby, waves of seashells, created by embedding shells into wet, color-tinted drywall compound, wash up along the wall.

TIKI HUT VALANCE

PALM TREE PHOTOS

CROCHET FRINGE

SISAL RUG

the existing furniture, lighting, flooring, and other elements. This plan helps her to visualize the finished room, check for traffic flow, and to decide on purchases and projects.

While Nadia's floor plans are beautifully drawn, many plans begin more simply, with the room measurements and features, such as windows, doors, and electrical outlets, drawn onto graph paper. Furniture to remain in the room or to be purchased or built is also measured or estimated, and the measurements are used to make graph-paper cutouts that can be manipulated on the room layout. From the finished floor plan, room elevations, which further detail the room's aesthetic, are created to provide a visual reference.

To transform this tired living room into a tropical paradise, Nadia took her design-theme cues from Jack's love for the beach. Function comes first, however, and because the carpet was in poor condition, Nadia replaced it with an easy-care surface: bamboo flooring. Aesthetically this was an obvious choice; the bamboo fit perfectly with her theme. In addition bamboo flooring is more durable than hardwood and is more environmentally sustainable: Bamboo, which is technically a grass, reaches harvestable size

"My rooms always have a vibrant colorful feeling...The rooms I design are more of a collection of new and old." — *Nadia Geller*

OUTDOOR UMBRELLA

PAPER LANTERNS

BAMBOO DIVIDER

GRASS SKIRTING

NEW STOOLS

DOUBLE DECKER CAT HAMMOCK

DINING AREA

NG 04

Sheltered under an outdoor umbrella, the custom picnic table and matching benches suggest a beach picnic. The cushions on the benches are made from foam sheets, available in several thicknesses from crafts and fabric stores, that are covered with fabric.

## Hawaiian-Shirt Pillow

1 Push a 12- or 16-inch square pillow form into the shirt body, against the shoulder seams. Pin the front and back of the shirt together around the perimeter of the form and leave an opening at the bottom. Remove the form and turn the shirt wrong side out. Carefully transfer the pins to the wrong side to mark the seam; sew, leaving a 6-inch opening at the bottom. Trim excess shirt fabric to ½-inch and turn right side out.

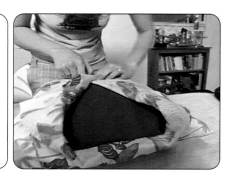

**2** Insert the pillow form and cut neck-liner fabric to match the pillow form dimensions; insert the liner into the opening to check placement. Pin the upper edge of the liner fabric to the base of the collar, right sides together; remove the form and turn wrong side out; sew. Pin the liner to the shoulder and side seams; sew. Turn right side out; insert the pillow form; slip stitch the opening at the bottom.

# "Turn things inside out; look inside of things…Pillows, drapes, and valances are surprisingly easy." – *Leslie Segrete*

every three to five years. The stalks are cut into strips, processed, and glued into planks that can be installed like hardwood or laminate flooring. Prefinished bamboo flooring can cost $4 to $8 per square foot, but Internet sources advertise prices as low as $1.99 per square foot.

Nadia also had to consider whether she would interpret the tropical design literally, with beach-theme objects and materials, or symbolically, with colors and shapes that merely would suggest the beach—for example, a color scheme of faded aqua, sky blue, and sandy taupe and graphic tone-on-tone wave-pattern upholstery. Nadia opted for the literal interpretation and designed projects such as the Tiki hut valances, Hawaiian-shirt throw pillows, and picnic table and benches for the space.

### Theme in Color

Color is a major part of any design plan, and it was especially so here. To determine the color palette, Nadia looked to items from the

**OPPOSITE** Roommate Arwen won the aquarium coffee table by answering a quiz question correctly. The candles were created by placing a wick in each coconut shell and pouring melted wax inside. **RIGHT** Nadia found vintage Hawaiian shirts secondhand, but new shirts would work just as well.

## *Choosing Color & Fabrics*

With so many options available for decorating, sometimes it's hard to know where to start when selecting colors and fabrics for a room. Often a multi-color fabric—such as the bench fabric shown *right*—is a good starting point for choosing other colors and fabrics. Note how the earthy tan, red, and green colors in the patterned bench fabric have influenced the choice of the solid fabrics used on other elements. This proven method for mixing multiple fabrics in a room ensures a coordinated palette and continuity for the evolving room design.

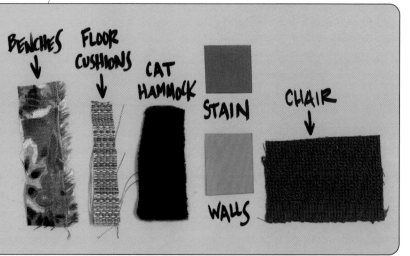

BENCHES · FLOOR CUSHIONS · CAT HAMMOCK · STAIN · CHAIR · WALLS

"I want to do this for Jack, for being such a supportive friend for so many years." –*Arwen*

# TIKI ENTERTAINMENT SHELF

past, such as vintage Hawaiian shirts, old postcards, and tourist memorabilia. From these reference points she pulled out a riot of 1950s colors, including aqua, lime, forest, red, coral, tan, and brown. She used these hues to choose paint, fabrics, and accessories, which came together to create a playful retro look.

When using reference items to guide your decorating choices, remember that the same colors can evoke different periods or eras, depending on their proportion. For example, aqua accented with black was a popular color scheme from the 1950s. Black accented with aqua or its darker cousins turquoise or teal, however, may create an '80s look.

Geography, culture, and personal experiences all affect how people perceive colors, so it's important to experiment with different color combinations before proceeding with the actual selections for the room. Being aware of color nuances and using them properly strengthens the final design.

**LEFT** Unfinished lumber and bamboo were used for the projects to keep the room casual. **ABOVE AND OPPOSITE** Nadia's design plan includes colorful elevation drawings, marker sketches of projects, fabric swatches, and before photos. These items help her to visualize the room and communicate her ideas to the team.

PALM TREE PARADISE

SEATING AREA

CUSHIONS

BENCHES

HAMMOCK

STAIN

WALLS

CHAIR

Before

Before

SIDE TABLE

PALM TREE PHOTOS

HAWAIIAN SHIRT PILLOW

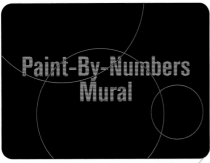

## Paint-By-Numbers Mural

1 Create a detailed drawing or photocopy a design for the mural. Draw a grid over the design with a pencil, to separate it into manageable parts. Generally, a 1-inch square on the drawing equals a 1-foot square on the wall, but make adjustments as needed for your drawing and wall size. Use a snap line to divide the wall into coordinating grids.

## "I give bamboo a thumbs-up! It cuts nicely and is drilled and screwed easily. [It] looked great on the finished product." – *Jason Cameron*

### Outstanding Objects

Nadia played up the beach theme by using objects that would instantly evoke images of the tropics. For example, she rejected typical dining room furniture in favor of a picnic-style table and benches complete with an outdoor patio umbrella. The table and benches pack a design punch without sacrificing function.

To make the table and matching benches, Jason used large green bamboo stalks cut to length for the legs. The tabletop and bench seats consist of a 1×4 framework covered with more 1×4s placed side by side; spacers separate the boards while attaching them to the framework. Jason cut a hole in the top of the table for the umbrella pole.

Items from the 1950s give Nadia's beach theme a vintage look. Kitschy cocktail umbrellas embellish picture frames, and photographs printed in sepia tones and then color-washed recall old hand-tinted postcards. The repeated use of the windswept palm tree motif gives continuity to the space and shores up the design theme.

### Big Idea

Because this room has no important architectural features, Nadia had to create one element that would dominate visually. In keeping with the playful design scheme, she devised a dramatic, paint-by-numbers wall mural to serve as the focal point of the room.

Her inspiration came from vintage graphics. She transferred the design to the wall and painted it using colors that complement the new furniture and fabrics. The grand scale of the mural captures the eye and downplays the low ceiling and painted paneling.

The horizontal lines that dominate the scenic mural echo the lines of nearby built-in furniture. Together these elements create a calm vista and evoke a sense of harmony.

LEFT AND OPPOSITE **Interesting textures, such as the grass-skirt material hung on the entertainment shelving and the Tiki hut valances, soften the room. The valances have a skeleton framework made from lightweight lumber. The corner entertainment unit was constructed to hold about 200 pounds, perfect for heavy televisions and electronic equipment.**

**2** Transfer the drawing to the wall, one grid section at a time. Assign a number to every color represented in the drawing. Mark the numbers on the corresponding cans of paint and sections on the wall. Note: Pencil lines will show through some colors of paint, so use chalk (or erase the pencil marks before painting). Paint the sections accordingly.

# John Bruce— Untitled

## Film student Ryan describes his roommate, Cassie, as his friend and inspiration. He's asked the WYWO team to turn a plain room into her artist's retreat.

**C**ollege rentals are known for having little personality, and the Savannah apartment living room of students Ryan and Cassie was a typical blank canvas. White space is usually not a problem for the *While You Were Out* team members, who are well-trained in both applied and fine arts. But because this student apartment came with rules to obey, the team was forced to enliven the room without painting the walls or permanently changing the structure.

After sending Cassie to Atlanta on a trumped-up search for potential theater sites for one of his future plays, Ryan welcomes the *While You Were Out* team to the apartment. Host Evan Farmer and carpenters Leslie Segrete and Andrew Dan-Jumbo trust that designer John Bruce will have creative projects to fabricate for this artistic transformation.

*Before*

John describes his plan as a "surreal assemblage." He explains that his design for the room was influenced by automatic writing, a surrealistic technique for unpremeditated, free-association writing, and Dada, an early 20th-century art movement that aimed to ridicule the culture through absurd performances.

To make an impact on the barren space,

John designed an easy-to-remove, large-scale wall treatment and a fabric room divider. He also designed freestanding movable furniture, including an "exquisite corpse" occasional table (the head, body, and legs are on separate sections of the table; see *pages 69 and 73*) and a kaleidoscope end table.

### Temporary Treatments

Rental units often have strict policies that forbid permanent physical changes to the walls or structure, so adding personality can be especially challenging. The wall-of-words project that John created for this space is a creative way to add color, drama, and personal expression. It's nondamaging and removable; even better, the project is inexpensive and fun.

Lightbulbs dipped in silver paint hang from extensions created using parts found in a home-improvement lighting department. The sewing machine, a WYWO prize, will be put to good use by art student Cassie.

John started with art paper featuring a pleasing blue and white cloud pattern. The paper provides an ethereal backdrop for bold black letters that spell out the words of a poem by the English poet Lord Byron.

The impact of this wall art is dramatic, but creating it was relatively simple. Rectangular pieces of art paper were applied to the wall with edges overlapping. Then self-stick letters, available on the Internet and from arts and crafts stores, were applied; painter's tape was used as a guide to keep the lines of text level.

The obligatory white walls that remain balance the big-impact wall treatment and stand back so John's other creations get due attention. (Neutral walls in a museum showcase fine artwork in much the same way.)

John chose not to hang the expected framed art or mirror over the fireplace. Instead, he purchased 11 fake, bright red cardinals and a single contrasting blue bird from a crafts store. Evan wired them onto removable hooks placed in a grid above the fireplace. The bold red birds "pop" against the white wall, but it's the repetition of a single element that makes this display so effective. This "designer's trick" adds visual impact and importance to simple or otherwise unremarkable items.

Like all good artwork, the display stimulates thought: With all but one bird facing in the same direction, the arrangement becomes a commentary on a freethinker's life. Inexpensive to

LEFT, ABOVE, OPPOSITE The hinged table was custom-made by Andrew, but a ready-made table could be adapted for this project. The purchased tiles are grouted according to manufacturer's directions and the painted army men glued down and covered with an acrylic sheet mounted on acrylic-tube corner pieces.

Please Have

A Seat

## Curtain Divider

**1** Screw large eye hooks into the upper door frame, approximately 4 inches from the wall, on both sides of the door opening. If the screws will be installed directly into drywall, use a ceiling anchor kit. Run cable through the eye hooks. Secure the ends of the cabling by wrapping the cable around the outer edge of the eye hook and back onto itself; wrap several times with heavy wire to hold.

**2** Measure the opening and sew a lightweight, sheet-like drapery to fit. Finish all seams using a French-seam technique, a serger, or a zigzag stitch. Machine hem the drapery equally on all sides. Do this by folding the edges under ¼ inch and pressing, and then folding again 1 inch and pressing. Carefully sew the hem using a hemstitch or by straight stitching ⅛ inch from the upper hem fold.

# "Andrew and I were there to make John's visions come to life. He came up with the most imaginative projects...The results were amazing." – *Leslie Segrete*

install, the display can be changed in a few minutes. When the renters move on, the hooks can be easily removed, leaving no marks on the wall.

### Drapery Dividers

The apartment living room faces the kitchen, often a cluttered and busy place. To make the living room more inviting and to hide the kitchen clutter, a curtain divider was installed. Wire, strung from hooks screwed into the door-frame molding, creates a taut line that supports quick-sew, cotton-blend draperies hung from drapery clips.

Draperies like these, or those made from sheets, are a good solution for temporary housing, because the large widths of fabric can be refashioned into draperies, slipcovers, or pillow covers for future homes.

### Flexible Furniture

The two tables that John designed and Andrew built are functional pieces, but they're also inspired by works of art. The "exquisite corpse" table consists of two movable sections, each featuring a portion of a Charlie Chaplin-like figure. The section featuring the head is made from mosaic tiles; the torso section consists of toy army men painted white, light gray, dark gray, and black. The varying stances of the army men provide a subtle textural shift and, along with the change in gray

**OPPOSITE AND RIGHT** Red accents used judiciously draw attention to selected objects in the room and move the eye through the space. The bird display over the fireplace showcases designer John Bruce's dry wit.

**BUT THESE A**
**ULD NOT PASS AWAY**
**OUGH THEE ART H**
**ECAY, THEE N SLAVE RS**
**BI RTH; THE HIGH ,THE**
**D BE- AND SHA LL, SUR VIV**
**TY, LOOK FORTH IN THE**
**ERI SHA BLY PURE BEYO**
**WIT HI TS CRY STAL FA**
**M OUNT A IN S VIE W TH**
**A CE IT SCLE A R DE PTI**
**BE I STOO MUCHMAN H**

R
AN D
FOR
ND
MOU
OR
UN'S
ND AI
CE,
ST
YI EL
ERE T

## Wall of Words

**1** Use removable double-stick tape to adhere several sheets of heavy or durable art paper to the wall. If the paper is lightweight, overlap the edges of the sheets ¼ inch on all sides. For wall-to-wall installations, use a straightedge and sharp mat knife to trim away excess paper at the corners and ceiling and along the base molding.

# "We have been each other's inspirations...I owe her my life, and more." – Ryan

scale, give movement, or a hint of life, to the corpse.

The legs of the corpse are not part of the table at all. They are made from two separate box pillows sewn from black, white, and gray fabric; they hang from hooks, just above the surface of the table. Another box pillow hangs above the legs and features a machine-embroidered message: "Please Have A Seat."

The kaleidoscope table (shown to the right of the overstuffed chair on *page 72*) is an experimental design made from a garbage can, a large tube, plywood, and mirrors. John warned Andrew before he started on the table that the project "could fail horribly," but Andrew's persistence paid off. The finished table looks like many round end tables, but when you look through the surface glass, the inside sparkles like a kaleidoscope.

In addition to the custom pieces, some of the original furniture was updated to fit with the new look. John had the coffee table and desk painted black to provide visual weight. Leslie reupholstered the overstuffed chair using a high-sheen stretchy knit.

## Artistic Accessories

To finish the space the team installed accessories that would rival the focal-point art of an ordinary room. A framed translucent photograph of Cassie and Ryan makes a creative fireplace screen. Not intended for use when the fireplace is in use, the screen is illuminated from behind by a small, low-watt uplight.

A collage that Ryan created from pop graphics and typefaces fills in the blank space under the kitchen counter. Ready-made, prestretched canvas works well for a collage foundation and is available in a variety of sizes.

**LEFT Shiny spandex, an unlikely upholstery fabric, was stretched over an overstuffed chair. The rounded shape contrasts with and softens the horizontal and vertical lines of the space and makes the room more inviting.**

## What's an Exquisite Corpse?

Exquisite corpse is a method used to assemble a collection of unrelated words, phrases, or images from two or more people. The technique is based on an old French parlor game called "Le cadavre exquis boira le vin nouveau," (The exquisite corpse will drink the young wine), also known as "Consequences."

In the original game, one player would write down a phrase, then fold the paper to cover most of the words and pass it to the next player, who would then add his or her contribution. No one would see the collective work until all were finished. Later, surrealists used the technique with images, assigning a different portion of the human body to each player.

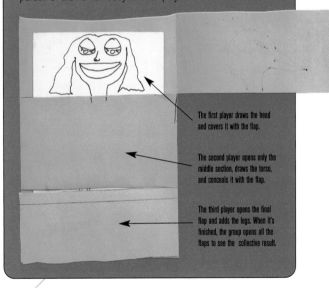

The first player draws the head and covers it with the flap.

The second player opens only the middle section, draws the torso, and conceals it with the flap.

The third player opens the final flap and adds the legs. When it's finished, the group opens all the flaps to see the collective result.

2 Measure the height of the tallest letter to be applied to the wall. Use this measurement to determine the line height for the text. Measure from the floor up to the first line where type will be placed and make a small pencil mark. Do this across the wall in several places. Connect the pencil marks with narrow painter's tape. Repeat for every line of type.

3 Measure the width of an average-size letter as a guide for determining approximate word length and placement. In light pencil, mark flag points, such as the start of sentences, the beginning and ending of words, and where punctuation occurs. Peel self-adhesive letters from the backing paper and apply just above the painter's tape. When finished, remove the painter's tape.

# Comfortable Caravan

## Tent-inspired striped walls, playful paint treatments, and exotic accessories turn an average family room into a well-coordinated retreat.

**n**early every home has at least one room that isn't living up to its potential. At Karen and Harem's Virginia home, the family room was the household underachiever. The room had builder-white walls and boring furniture, which Karen wanted to change. Her goal was to make the room more comfortable for her hardworking and dedicated husband, who had agreed to move the family to Virginia even though it would mean a 10-hour weekend commute for a few years until his retirement. To say thank you, she wanted to give him a room where he could relax with his family and truly feel at home.

Before

Designer Mark Montano, host Evan Farmer, and carpenters Ali Barone and Andrew Dan-Jumbo magically made over the space and gave it a fresh, custom-designed look. The secret to their professional results? Hard work, fabulous paint treatments, color-matched fabrics, knockout accessories, and a classic approach to interior design.

### The Big Idea

Mark took inspiration from caravans of the past to create his "big idea" for the room. A tent-stripe paint treatment and a tent-flap border at the ceiling line give instant personality to the room. Striped draperies and tent-flap cornices translate the paint treatment in fabric, adding dimension and softness. The caravan theme also inspired two recurring motifs, elephants and palms. The careful repetition of one or two motifs is a tried-and-true way to establish continuity and unity in a room.

The color palette is predominantly yellow and green with a healthy dose of off-white to keep the look fresh. The colors appear in different intensities, combinations, and quantities and on a selection of materials, from smooth cotton to a highly textured rug, from the wall paint to the beads that embellish candles. This keeps the room coordinated but still interesting and not overly matched.

To meet the functional needs of the family, Mark planned for comfortable seating,

Caravan-inspired stripes painted on the walls
instantly set the stage for a retreat. The draperies
were created by sewing strips of fabric together. The
slat coffee table and shapely leaning shelf were
carpentry projects created especially for the room.

## Coffee Table

1 On kraft paper, draw a full-size pattern for the elongated C-shape table legs. Make the table about as tall as your sofa seat and two-thirds to three-fourths the sofa length. Transfer the pattern to plywood, medium-density fiberboard (MDF), or boards pinned and glued together. (Andrew used three separate pieces of wood for his table-leg section.)

including enough for guests, strategically placed tables, and a comfy spot for resting weary feet. Luckily for Karen and Harem, they won a new sofa, chair, and ottoman as quiz prizes during the show. To complement these, Andrew Dan-Jumbo crafted tables and an hourglass display shelf.

The coffee table and end tables are Montano/Dan-Jumbo works of art. Two elongated C-shape side pieces provide the framework for a series of evenly spaced wood slats that form the top and ends. The light oak stain picks up the color of the mantel shelf and Queen Anne-style side chairs. The wall shelf is cut in an hourglass shape from MDF (medium-density fiberboard). Routed channels in the back board hold curved oak shelves for showcasing decorative accessories.

After establishing the creature comforts, Mark focuses on aesthetics. The room had attractive architectural features: a fireplace on an angled wall, nicely trimmed windows, and French doors. But as in most family rooms, the television took center stage. Instead of fighting this fact, Mark embraced it and flanked the oversize television with draperies. The treatment softens the hard edges of the TV and incorporates the big box into the room.

## Star Treatments

When the budget is tight, paint treatments—on furnishings as well as walls—can add impact for relatively few dollars. Mark's striped treatment is time-consuming but easy to execute. It starts with a foundation of light yellow applied to all walls with a roller. When the paint is thoroughly dry, use painter's tape to mark the

**OPPOSITE Room colors are repeated in the framed art. Create your own originals by squirting crafts paint onto a page and then folding the page onto itself. ABOVE Evan used recycled wood, left over from projects, and twine to make candleholders.**

2 Rout the upper inside edge of the table legs to create a rabbet, or groove, where the slats can be attached. Begin and end the groove to create a foot for the table, approximately 5 inches high. Cut slats from 1/4×2-inch boards to the length desired. Space slats evenly along the rabbet using a spacer made from leftover wood. Use finishing nails to attach the slats to the legs.

3 Sand the table to remove rough areas, starting with a medium-grit sandpaper and moving to a fine-grit one. (The table should feel completely smooth.) Use a tack cloth to remove sanding dust. If desired, stain the table and finish with two coats of polyurethane. Follow the manufacturer's directions for all products.

placement of narrow green stripes and medium-width darker yellow stripes. Short rollers make quick work of applying the additional colors. The tent-flap treatment at the ceiling was created using a template cut from cardboard.

For the side chair, mirror, and shelf, Mark used a combed finish. This treatment uses a gel stain rather than paint so the wood grain or previous stain can be seen through the top layer. You can create the squiggly lines in the wet gel stain with a trowel, as was used here, or with notched cardboard or a wide-tooth comb.

## Custom Seams

Decorators and designers often order custom pillows, draperies, tablecloths, and other fabric items made specifically for the rooms they are creating. Custom designs are an important part of high-end decorator looks, but they can also break the bank.

To get a custom look for the draperies and still stay within the *While You Were Out* budget, Mark selected a mix of solid and patterned fabrics; he then had them cut into strips and pieced to make his own custom-stripe fabric. This trick is especially useful if you wish to use a mix of colors that you can't find in ready-loomed fabrics from chain or local fabric stores. It's also an ideal way to create or reinforce a color scheme.

Another way to combine fabrics for a custom look is by color-blocking. Mark used this technique on a hanging lampshade, shown on *page 80*. He started with two $19 shades and spray-glued yellow and green solid fabric to them so the front and back are different colors. He then hot-glued the two shades together, bottom rim to bottom rim, matching up opposite colors on each shade. Ribbon covers the seams.

Trims, cording, and piping also offer ways to customize accessories. Mark used dark brown ribbon to embellish pillows for the sofa to get the look he wanted.

## Designer Details

Professional designers spend hours searching for the right art and accessories because they know that these details can turn a pleasant room into a powerhouse. For people on a budget, creating custom-made accessories and art can be as easy as a

**LEFT Leaf motifs, cut from photography gels, were attached to the windows with silver hot glue. OPPOSITE MDF offers a smooth surface for paint or in this case, a gel stain. Unlike regular stains, gel stains provide even coverage for this material.**

"I love him very much and he's a good daddy and a good husband!" —*Karen*

# "I always go to the 'oops' paint section and try to color-match for $5 as opposed to $20 [a gallon]. I often get lucky." —Ali Barone

trip to the hardware or arts and crafts store. To make the dramatic floor mirror *right*, Ali started with a sheet of MDF, which she comb-painted using a gel stain; then she glued down mirror squares. Instead of mirror tiles you could attach a door mirror, using a strong adhesive, and trim around the mirror with moldings for a more traditional look.

To make customized candles, Karen and Evan took inexpensive plain pillars, heated the surface with a hair dryer, then rolled the warmed candle in a pan of tiny beads. The candleholders were created from leftover wood pieces wrapped with twine. The team couldn't invest in expensive paintings, so they created art from crafts paints squeezed onto heavy paper. Folding and unfolding the paper produced Rorschach-inspired paintings that were framed and hung over the mantel.

These projects required only ordinary materials. Mark also adapted materials intended for other purposes. For example, to add color to the French doors, he used photography gels, commonly used by professional photographers. These translucent plastic-like sheets come in a variety of colors and can be cut into shapes and glued to windows to create the look of stained glass.

---

**OPPOSITE The finished room glows with the addition of a hanging lamp. Mark used spray glue to attach fabric to two plain lampshades, then he hot-glued them together and covered his seams with ribbon. RIGHT The large mirror can be secured with picture hardware and wire, if desired.**

## Leaning Mirror

**1** The mirror back is made from one 4x8-foot sheet of MDF (medium-density fiberboard) cut to 4x6 feet. Sand all sides of the back board and wipe the sanding dust off with a tack cloth. Measure and mark a pencil line for a 7-inch border around the perimeter of the board. Use painter's tape to mask just inside the line, so the outer edge can be painted.

**2** Paint gel stain onto the outer edge of the board. While the gel is still wet, drag a trowel over the surface to make a squiggle design; see photo, *above right*. Use the gel according to the manufacturer's directions. Allow the gel to dry thoroughly; then adhere the mirrors. (Note: Only gel stains will work on MDF; avoid using regular stains. For another option, use paint.)

**3** Measure and mark the back board for the mirror placement. To adhere the mirrors to the board, squeeze caulk (check mirror manufacturer for suggested product name) in an even application onto the back side of the mirror; see photo, *left*. Turn the mirror over and carefully set it in place. Press lightly with the palm of your hand to mount. Let dry.

# Take Eames, Fire!

## A small space goes from mundane to modern: Innkeeper Sherri convinces the WYWO team to transform living quarters as a surprise for her husband.

**S**herri and Marshall are big fans of *While You Were Out* and often enjoyed the show together in their cramped living space at the back of the bed-and-breakfast they own in St. Augustine, Florida. According to Sherri, late one night after they had watched an episode and Marshall had gone to bed, she secretly applied for a *While You Were Out* makeover online. She wanted to surprise Marshall with a masculine retreat to thank him for unselfishly agreeing to a drastic lifestyle change that allowed her to pursue her dream of being an innkeeper.

The *While You Were Out* team agreed to take on the disorderly digs knowing full well from the photos and videotape that this would be a demanding space.

*Before*

They were confident, however, that designer John Bruce would deliver an exciting transformation. Carpenters Jason Cameron and Ali Barone and host Evan Farmer stood by ready to execute his plan.

The room posed some design challenges common to small spaces that must serve a variety of functions. Besides being a living, dining, and storage space, it's also the backdoor entry to the inn. Because this is where deliveries are made and groceries are carried through to the kitchen, smooth daytime traffic flow is important. But at night, when the innkeepers have time to relax, they want a cozy retreat for television viewing, reading, and eating.

### Directing Traffic

Studying the floor plan gives clues to problem areas in any home. In this case, the main hallway runs through the center of the L-shape space, with a bathroom on one side and a large support wall on the other. The small hallway is a busy traffic area during the day, and unfortunately it offers back-door visitors and seated guests a clear view of the bathroom.

To improve the traffic flow and eliminate a potential safety hazard, John removed a lightweight, freestanding television shelf from the center of the room. The

The walls were painted yellow-green to brighten the room and to set off the rich wood tones. Sleek furniture, selected and designed to keep the traffic areas clear, makes the room appear larger. Textures on the lamp and leather rug keep the room visually interesting.

television moved into a new built-in unit that John designed. The unit looks grand, but it is actually sheets of plywood screwed into the walls on each side of the hallway. A hole cut into the plywood provides access to shelves that hold the television and electronic equipment. The face of the plywood is embellished with an applied wood design to give it a furniture look. While blocking the small hallway with the unit does slow down traffic a bit, people are forced to go through the larger dining area, which offers more elbow room. This solution also solved the problem of excess furniture clutter and improved the view from the sitting area.

## Designing Details

John's design plan, inspired by the warm, modern aesthetic of midcentury designers Ray and Charles Eames, calms the busy space with organic materials and a streamlined style. Furniture is kept simple; only a few hardworking pieces—an armless sofa, a classic Eames leather-and-wood chair and ottoman, a petite pedestal table and stackable chairs, and a sculptural floor lamp—

LEFT Designed by John, an armless sofa made from plywood is a clean-lined addition to the room. The foam cushion is covered with upholstery fabric. OPPOSITE Contemporary cylinder lampshades are made from a purchased Kona wood rug and a sheet of wood veneer.

# Kona Wood Floor Lamp

1 Spray-paint the stand and base of an old floor lamp (John used dark red primer for the base coat and top coat.) Allow the paint to dry thoroughly between each coat. Cut sheets of grass-textured art paper to fit around the base and hot-glue in place, overlapping as needed to cover the entire stand. Mount a new wire lampshade frame, or use an old one with the fabric cover removed.

2 Use a ready-made Kona wood rug (John found this one in a kitchen chain store) to make the shade. Wrap the rug around a wire lampshade and mark where it overlaps. Cut the excess material from the rug, using wire cutters or heavy-duty shears. Wrap the rug around the lampshade frame and wire the upper edge of the rug to the frame. Connect the two ends of the rug together with wire.

"WYWO isn't merely interior decorating—it's more like installation art and experimental theater on a downtown budget." – *John Bruce*

are chosen to outfit the room. Because the major pieces are relatively low-slung, clean-lined, and visually lightweight, the room feels spacious.

Light-color wood grains in a limited range of tones make the room seem larger, yet offer enough variety to entertain the eye. A less-is-more strategy keeps accessories to a minimum, reinforcing the clean, uncluttered look, while the play of curvilinear lines against straight lines keeps the eye moving around the room.

### Simplifying Surfaces

To reduce visual clutter, John replaced some of the window's busy floral pattern with hollow-core plastic material, cut to fit snugly inside the panes. The frosted effect calms the room.

In keeping with the clean aesthetic of the Eameses, John detailed the face of the television unit with a simple geometric design created from chunks and strips of wood. This textural change provides visual interest that's more subtle than a busy pattern or a loud color. John also devised a modern facelift for the dowdy, louvered closet doors.

ABOVE AND OPPOSITE **Textured art papers, wood veneers, and enlarged color photos of grass make a dramatic door design.** RIGHT **Cork flooring replaces the old dining room carpet. The natural material blends well with the multiple wood tones in the room.**

"...because he has supported me in living my dream of owning a bed-and-breakfast."
—Sherri

# "A well-designed room has to evoke a feeling while remaining balanced and functional." – *Ali Barone*

The television unit and the closet doors were transformed to the new clean style with readily available materials. The size and placement of the decorative wood pieces on the television unit were plotted on graph paper; then the pieces were glued and tacked in place. For the closet doors, John used tagboard inserts and covered them with a collage of organic-inspired papers, wood veneers, color photocopies of grass, and balsa wood strips.

Flooring in all of the areas except under the dining room table was hard-surface, a durable choice for high-traffic areas. The dining room carpet texture and color made the room look chopped up and emphasized its small size; the uneven floor underneath posed a hazard, so it had to go.

After the carpet was removed, the floor was corrected with a floor-leveling product; when combined with water, this product pours on as a thin

**OPPOSITE** A chunky side table cut from exotic wood stands next to an armless sofa. The Eames lounge chair and the leather rug (shown *right*) were prizes. **RIGHT** The television unit was built to fit into the doorway.

## Entertainment Unit

**1** This unit, built into the door frame, consists of a plywood, boxlike structure with compartments for the television and electronic equipment. The structure was suspended between the two side walls and bolted in place. To figure the size of the compartments, measure the television and electronic equipment and allow enough room to move them in and out, plus enough depth for air circulation.

**2** Plywood sheets face the unit and provide a level surface for attaching various wood pieces. Use graph paper to plot the design before cutting the wood pieces. Attach the pieces to the plywood with wood glue and finishing nails. When completed, the unit can be stained or left natural. Finish with polyurethane, following the manufacturer's directions.

# "[We] show how creativity can take the place of money... It's all about creativity and thinking outside the box." — *Evan Farmer*

mixture, settles onto the uneven surface, and dries. In this case, narrow boards were placed along the perimeter of the space to hold the watery mix in place while it set. When the leveler was dry, the new flooring was installed according to the manufacturer's directions; transition strips were used to connect the flooring to the original floor.

Matching the original floor was impossible, so John selected cork floor tiles in a color similar in intensity to the existing flooring material. By selecting a hard-surface material that complements the original floor, John improved the visual flow within the space.

**RIGHT** The built-in television unit facade has a textural design that Evan made with various types and sizes of wood. Before beginning the project, John plotted the placement of the pieces on graph paper for Evan to use as a map. The wood was glued and nailed onto the plywood backing, then sealed with clear polyurethane.

## Who Are Charles and Ray Eames?

Charles and Ray Eames were a husband-and-wife design team with a mission: They wanted to bring the "good life" to the average American in the postwar 1950s. They created high-quality, affordable modern furniture, such as the Eames lounge chair used in this room. As design pioneers, they worked with new materials and methods to create sleek-looking furniture, including chairs made from bent plywood and Fiberglas. The Eameses' *Powers of Ten*, a film dealing with the relative size of things in the universe, inspired John Bruce's photographs of grass that appear on the folding doors (see *pages 86 and 87*).

# Suite
# Dreams

The *While You Were Out* team shows you how easy it is to turn a boring bedroom into a private and very personal retreat.

# Midnight
# Cowgirl

**Rodeo champion Tee Woolman ropes the** *While You Were Out* **gang into helping him surprise his wife, Jacqui, with a Texas-size bedroom makeover.**

ee Woolman and son Walker, 13, weren't sure what to expect when they asked for a fast-action bedroom makeover. These real-life cowboys are more familiar with riding and roping than with decorating, but they agreed they wanted to do something especially nice for wife and mom, Jacqui, to thank her for everything she has done for them over the years.

So while Jacqui was off being filmed for a bogus documentary, the father and son got help from designer Chayse Dacoda, host Evan Farmer, and carpenters Jason Cameron and Ali Barone. Chayse had done her homework; after studying a videotape of the room, she created a design plan to transform the space.

The room had many positives, but it also had several problems common to new-house master bedrooms. It was a large, boxy space with white walls, nondescript woodwork, no important architectural features, and an expanse of plain, low-nap carpet. To sum it up, the space was missing personality; in fact, it looked more like an office than a bedroom retreat. Undaunted, Chayse had solutions for adding character through color, furniture, and unusual fabrics. She also planned Western-theme projects to add personality to the space.

A rope canopy makes the bed a dramatic focal point in the room. Designer Chayse Dacoda attached the rope to the ceiling and framework with a staple gun.

"My perspective is constantly changing. I look at a space through my eyes, then the homeowner's eyes…" — *Chayse Dacoda*

### Set the Stage

Large rooms, especially personal spaces like this bedroom, need color to make them cozy and inviting. In this case, the room had been painted a cold neutral that made the space feel vacant and unwelcoming. To remedy this, Chayse chose two shades of warm tan that she and Ali mottled onto the walls to create a suede-like finish. The new paint treatment visually connects the wood tones in the room, thus reducing contrast. Although inexpensive, this treatment has major design impact: It encourages the eye to focus on the interior of the room instead of bouncing from dark to light elements on the walls. The result is a more relaxing and inviting space.

Suede-look paint is available from home-improvement centers and paint stores—usually at a premium price. To save money, Chayse made her own mix: two closely related paint colors (here, two midtone tans). She applied one shade in a small section (about 10 inches square) and then immediately painted the second shade next to it. She continued going back and forth between the colors and kept a blended, wet edge to eliminate hard lines.

**LEFT** Shelves above the closet doors provide additional storage and display space for cowboy hats. **OPPOSITE** The fabrics on the bed are a mix of faux suede and cow-pattern faux fur, natural-looking wovens with slubs, and a paisley that recalls the look of tooled leather.

## Fringed Bedcover

**1** To determine fabric yardage needed, measure the bed and allow for a drop to cover the bedskirt. You will need three fabrics: a red faux-suede foundation in the above measurements; a brown faux-suede fabric (to be cut 8 inches narrower and shorter than the foundation); and a paisley fabric (6-10 inches narrower and shorter than the bed). (Note: For wider beds stitch two fabric widths together.)

**2** Start by cutting the top appliqué from the paisley fabric, allowing an extra ½ inch on all sides for turning under. Center and pin the paisley fabric, right side up, on the brown-faux suede fabric and topstitch ¼ inch from edges. Center and pin the upper two layers to the foundation. Because the faux suede does not ravel, a hem is not needed. Topstitch about 5 inches from the brown fabric's edges.

**3** To fringe the bedcover, place painter's tape approximately 5 inches from the lower edge of the foundation fabric. Using sharp scissors, cut every ½ inch to make the fringe (see photo, *left*). To finish the sides of the bedcover, fringe the brown faux-suede fabric in the same manner to approximately ¼ inch below the topstitch line.

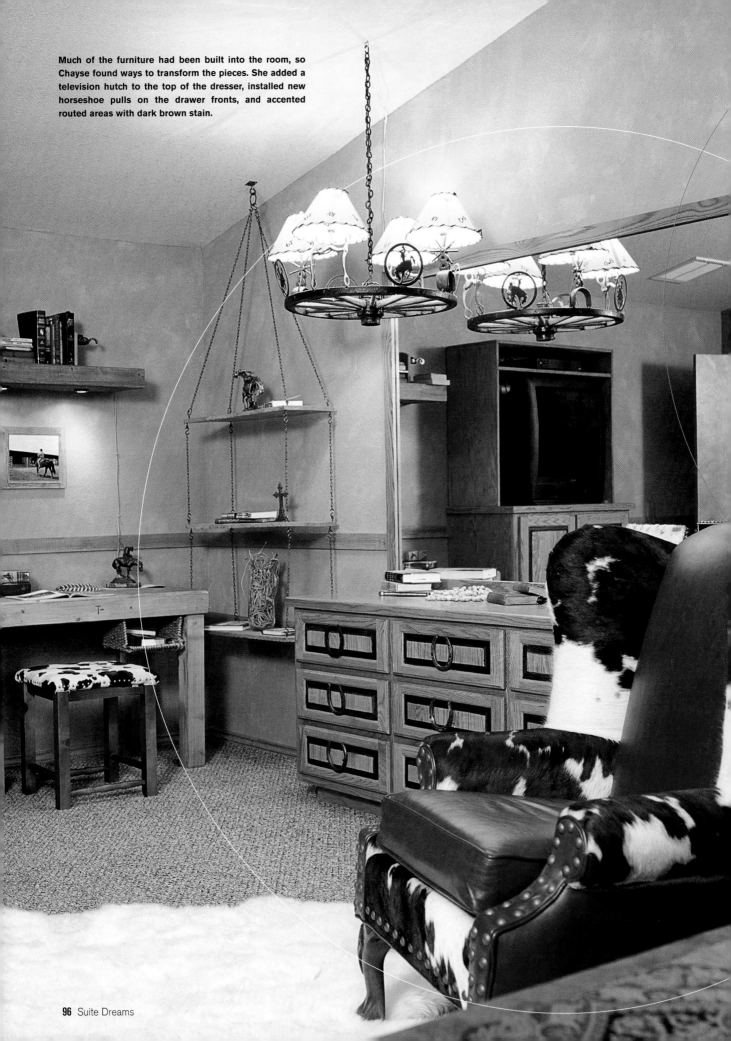

Much of the furniture had been built into the room, so Chayse found ways to transform the pieces. She added a television hutch to the top of the dresser, installed new horseshoe pulls on the drawer fronts, and accented routed areas with dark brown stain.

There's always time for horsing around on a *While You Were Out* set! Chayse, Evan, Ali, and Jason take a well-deserved break from a terrific Texas transformation.

After allowing the faux-finish paint treatment to dry, the team installed another wall treatment. Cedar planks were ripped lengthwise in half and nailed to the walls to create a rustic fence that adds texural interest and pushes the Western theme to the limit.

## Furniture That Fits

Obviously the furniture that fills the room must also fill the functional needs of the people who use it. But furniture also plays an important aesthetic role and expresses the owner's taste and personality. Often the easiest way to define the character of a space is to select and combine the right furniture. For example, a distinctively carved antique four-poster bed or a midcentury armless sofa upholstered in lime green can provide instant personality punch; however, such pieces can be quite costly.

In this room the problem wasn't which furniture should be purchased or built; it was finding ways to transform the built-in furniture that lined the walls. Even the platform bed was carpeted to match the floor. These pieces lacked the impact demanded by such a large space, but removing them was impossible because of time and budget constraints.

The positive side to this design dilemma was that the furniture was well-made, and the simple lines of the chests and nightstands provided a perfect foundation for adding Western-inspired treatments. Creative staining, new hardware, and clever embellishments turned ordinary furnishings into distinctive personality pieces.

Even a practical solution to hide the television was devised by building a cabinet to fit on top of the dresser, transforming it into an attractive entertainment unit.

To give the bed more importance and a grander scale, Chayse designed a wood four-poster and canopy frame that attaches directly to the bed platform. Heavy rope coiled on the ceiling and draped over the four corners of the frame completes the look.

Chayse added a hanging shelf made from distressed wood and a writing desk branded with the ranch's branding iron to the

**LEFT** The wagon-wheel light fixture was a prize. **OPPOSITE** In Chayse's design file she included sketches for the shelves and the horseshoe drawer pulls, two wovens, a faux fur, and a lightweight knit fabric, and paint chips for the colors she used on the walls.

"She is a really giving person, and I thought that she would enjoy this..."
—*Tee Woolman*

90°
angle attach

weld
po...

Horseshoe

4" long horiz
D...

Before

Before

shelf
above
closet

## Hanging Shelves

1 Cut three 1×12 boards to the desired length. (Shelves longer than 36 inches will require additional support chains.) Age the wood surfaces by gouging the edges with a chisel (see photo, *right*) and lightly denting the sides with a hammer or other heavy tool.

# "Pick a theme or a color palette and stick to it without the pressure that everything has to match perfectly…" — *Ali Barone*

furnishings. These additions enhance the new look while expanding the display and work space in the room.

## Inject Personality

Fabrics—in the form of bed linens, upholstery, draperies, and pillows—allow designers to create drama and emphasize a theme. Here fabrics include a dark red woven and faux cowhide. The suede-look fabric serves as the backdrop for an appliquéd coverlet. In the center of the faux suede, Ali appliquéd a large rectangle of paisley fabric that resembles tooled leather. The coverlet requires minimal sewing, and only a pair of scissors is needed to make the fringed edge.

Chayse picked up the Western theme with black and white cowhide-pattern fabric, which appears on a bolster, a stool seat, and the bedskirt. She also selected a wing chair, featuring a similar cowhide fabric, for a quiz prize. The large-scale, graphic print provides a pleasant contrast to smaller-scale patterns and solid fabrics and makes the room visually interesting.

Personal touches that reflect interests or family history make a space special. In her design for this room, Chayse acknowledged the couple's love for all things Western by using the ranch branding iron for the desk motif and installing two of Tee's rodeo competition trophy buckles as nightstand hardware.

She also created new framed art: She snapped photos of Tee on horseback and had them developed in sepia tones (this is easy to do with a digital camera and an in-store kiosk or your own computer). Chayse and Tee mounted the pictures on sandpaper mats whose edges they had torn and scorched for a rugged look. The effect is timeless and artistic, and the sepia tones harmonize with the new color palette to preserve the feeling of a restful retreat.

OPPOSITE **This dynamic chair was a prize that Chayse selected for the room. RIGHT The hanging shelf and the floating shelf above the desk offer display space for books and decorative accessories.**

2 Drill holes for heavy-duty eye hooks in the corners of the shelves. Install eye hooks on the upper and lower side of each shelf, spacing the two drill marks about 1 inch apart. Wipe with a clean tack cloth. Brush on golden-oak-tinted polyurethane in the direction of the wood grain. To minimize air bubbles in the polyurethane, allow it to rest in the can before using.

3 To hang the shelves screw four eye hooks into the ceiling, using ceiling anchors. (Refer to package instructions and product description to select the appropriate eye hooks and ceiling anchors for your situation.) Hang S hooks from the ceiling eye hooks and attach the chains. Then use more S hooks to connect the chain to the shelf eye hooks.

# Birmingham
# Imaginarium

## Drew is no ordinary big brother. His 16-year-old sister has outgrown her little-girl room. He asks the *While You Were Out* team to turn it into a mermaid's haven.

Before

**m**ichaela's room hasn't changed much since she was 7 years old and the family moved into the house. Michaela, however, has changed a lot. After losing a close friend to leukemia a few years ago, she has worked tirelessly to raise money for the American Cancer Society. This year, she and her friends have set a goal to earn $16,000 for the society, in honor of their sixteenth birthdays. Drew felt Michaela's efforts deserved a special reward, and the *While You Were Out* team agreed.

Designer Mark Montano surprised carpenters Leslie Segrete and Andrew Dan-Jumbo and host Evan Farmer with an out-of-this-world design. Taking inspiration from under the sea, he sketched a room that looks like a set for an underwater adventure. The focal point is a museum-quality quilt designed and stitched by the famous Gee's Bend quilting group. It features free-hanging "scales" in oceanic colors.

Although the look is pure fun, there's a practical side to the design. Fanciful elements such as a dock canopy and a ship's hull that protrudes from the corner offer extra storage space that will keep Michaela's room uncluttered. That's especially important in a room that's already brimming with shells, coral, net, and other seaside treasures.

### Lighten Up

The room is brightened in both attitude and physical characteristics. A fun and easy paint technique blends three colors of glaze in wavelike strokes on the walls. The swoops of color create a sense of movement. While the glaze is still wet, the team sprinkles on a bit of glitter, which sparkles like sunlight dancing on the ocean. Freehand drawings of coral are added later to give the room visual punch.

Instead of curtains, curvy strands cut from a shimmering vinyl shower curtain sway in the slightest breeze from the window. Hung from a minimal valance, they allow

Shells encrust the mirror frame and a valance made from MDF (medium-density fiberboard). The shells were attached with latex caulk.

# "In a bedroom, pick your bedding first and then your furniture and paint after that...Start with the focal point..." —*Mark Montano*

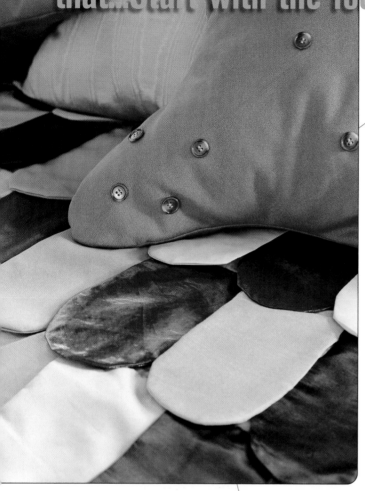

privacy but still let the sun shine in. The same treatment skirts the bed. The wavy cut of the material creates a feeling of movement similar to the gentle motion of seaweed in an ocean current.

To make the curtain and bed skirt, Mark unfolded the vinyl shower curtain panels to their full length. He then unfolded the panels vertically but only until they were thin enough for him to cut through. He found that by keeping the panels folded as much as possible, he reduced the number of cuts. This made the job go more quickly. Mark determined the length for the window and bed skirt by holding the panels in the proper position, making a mark at the bottom, and cutting off the excess. He then cut each panel into strips using pinking shears, so that each strip has "branches" that extend from the main vein. (See the photographs on *pages 108 and 109*.)

When the curtain strands were cut, Mark hung them from a curtain rod. For the bed skirt, Mark attached the strands to the upper edge of an inexpensive, ready-made bed skirt that had been placed over the box spring of the bed.

Mirrors are a necessity in any teen girl's room but not just for primping. Large mirrors—one draped with pearls and another rimmed with seashells—reflect light and make even a small room feel open and airy. To create a seashell mirror like the one shown *opposite*, purchase a mirror with a wide wood frame. Paint the frame a neutral color that will blend with the seashells. Cover the

---

**LEFT** A custom quilt, layered with U-shape scales in various shades of blue and green fabric, brings drama to the room. **OPPOSITE** The starfish pillows were made from a freehand pattern (draw one on kraft paper) and are accented with buttons.

## Dock Canopy

1 Measure the width of the bed and determine how far from the wall the canopy should protrude. Use these measurements to build a framework from 2x6-inch pine boards. Cover the frame with evenly spaced 1x4-inch boards. Note: The side connecting to the wall is made using boards, so it can be bolted into the wall; the side that protrudes has corners made from fence posts, cut to 18 inches high.

2 Apply stain and polyurethane to the canopy, if desired, according to the manufacturer's directions. To hang the canopy use heavy-gauge brackets anchored with at least ⅜-inch-diameter lag bolts. Be sure the bolt goes through the center of the ceiling joist. Bolt the legs of the pier to the wall studs behind the bed. Hang rope, fishnet, floats, and other appropriate sea items as desired.

frame with latex caulk and press the shells into the caulk. Glue on more layers of shells with industrial-strength glue or hot glue.

Wall and table lamps add soft light at night. Twigs spray-painted in coral and wired onto simple sconces take on the look of live coral. Fishbowls sitting on cube-shape light-boxes give a soft glow when the rest of the lights are low. Hidden inside the light-boxes are inexpensive uplights. Flat glass marbles and tiny mirror squares placed in the bottoms of the fishbowls reflect and refract the light from underneath.

## Store More

A dock over the bed takes the place of a canopy. Bolted to the wall studs and ceiling joists, it is draped with net, rope, glass floats, and other seaside items. The space between the dock and the ceiling provides storage for small items, out-of-season clothing, or books.

The hull of a ship protrudes from one corner of the room. Hidden inside is a flat-panel television that pulls down for viewing and slides back up when it's not being used. The ship bow has a wooden skeleton frame much like that of a real boat. Flexible wooden strips such as luaun are nailed over the skeleton to create the look of a real ship. A clever system of cables, brackets, and braces holds the hull in place.

---

**OPPOSITE A ship's hull breaks into the corner of the room and offers a hiding place for the flat-screen television. LEFT An old desk gets a new look. Several colors of spray paint overlap to mimic the murky deep. Shells were glued on to finish the theme.**

"MDF has been the saving grace on WYWO. It has allowed us to build items...and still remain within our budget." —*Andrew Dan-Jumbo*

Ship's Hull

1 Start with a template for the boat top. This is a Gothic-arch shape, cut from MDF (medium-density fiberboard). The boat top is where the ceiling mounting brackets are attached. Fold the template in half vertically and cut the center rib from MDF. If desired, cut a section from the center rib and mount a box, as shown at *left*, for the TV bracket. Glue and screw the center rib to the underside of the boat top.

2 Cut templates for three graduating horizontal ribs. These are in two parts (each a modified quarter circle) and connect to the center rib. This is the skeleton of the boat. Nail overlapping 1/16-inch boards or strips of luaun to sheathe the boat. (Stain and finish the strips before attaching for a two-tone look.) Finish with 1/8-inch boards around the upper edge and down the center of the boat. Mount to the ceiling joists.

# "Pick one color and then work with tones of the same color to give a room texture." —Leslie Segrete

An old desk gets a facelift when spray-painted with multiple colors that mimic the watery look of the wall treatment. Mark's technique is simple: If the desk is smooth or varnished, he sands the surface or treats it with a liquid sanding product so the decorative paint will adhere better. He paints the desk the desired base coat color, then chooses several contrasting colors of spray paint to spritz on quickly, one at a time, over the desk. It looks blotchy at first, but as he adds colors, they build up and overlap until the surface is completely covered with color. Finishing with a few light sprays of the first color pulls all the shades together. Clusters of shells glued around each drawer handle complete the look.

## Continuing Colors

Repeating the same colors, materials, and motifs throughout the room gives this design a cohesive look. Blue, green, turquoise, and coral show up on almost every piece. Shells and starfish find a home on the mirror, desk, lamps, and dressing table. Starfish also appear on the bed, as throw pillows with button barnacles.

Even the quilt takes on a maritime look. The free-hanging shapes resemble fish scales when the quilt takes its spot in this seaworthy room. Although this quilt was custom-designed and hand-sewn by a highly respected quilting guild, you can achieve a similar look using a prequilted base. Fit the base fabric to the bed and hem the edges. Make U-shape "scales" and hand- or machine-stitch them to the base.

Seaside accessories shore up the watery theme. The biggest impact comes from the dock canopy and boat hull simply because of their grand scale. These surprise elements set this ocean-theme room apart from the average teen bedroom.

---

**RIGHT** The draperies are made from vinyl shower curtains, cut into long coral-shapes with pinking shears or a pinking-edge rotary cutter. **OPPOSITE** The strips of vinyl can be glued to a curtain or tension rod or stapled to a wood strip mounted inside the window casing.

# "She does so much for other people...She's earned it. She's grown-up now..." —Drew

# The Southern Suite

## Lauren wants to pamper her mother with a bedroom redo. Despite heat, humidity, and other challenges, the WYWO team turns a catchall bedroom into a do-it-all suite.

auren's mother, Sandra, has had a rough year. The death of Sandra's father and the military deployment of Lauren's longtime boyfriend have put considerable stress on the family. Through it all, Sandra has been a pillar of strength for her family. Lauren calls the *While You Were Out* team to help her thank her mother by transforming her Lexington, Kentucky, master bedroom into a family suite.

*Before*

Designer Chayse Dacoda, host Evan Farmer, and carpenters Andrew Dan-Jumbo and Ali Barone agree that the room has great bones with good furniture. But it's still a long way from luxurious. A beautiful bed and dresser are the focal points of an otherwise bland room. The embossed wallpaper, which the family isn't fond of, loses all impact because it's flat white. The Queen Anne-style furniture stands uncomfortably against this stark backdrop.

To complicate matters, the family's computer and oversize computer hutch reside in the bedroom. This forces the space to become a homework center as well. As the family members all congregate around the computer, they linger and talk. While it's great to have a family gathering spot, there's one big problem: no seating.

### Personalize with Paint

Chayse proposes a design plan with Southern elegance. Glazed walls, custom-made fringed slipper chairs, and luxurious fabrics on the windows and bed will create a more elegant setting for the furniture.

The embossed wallpaper becomes a bonus instead of a drawback when the walls are treated to a soft off-white undercoat topped by a robin's egg blue glaze. Brushing and rubbing the glaze over the surface and allowing color to puddle in the crevices of the design gives the walls richness and depth.

Evan has one concern, however: The room is too feminine for a combination family room/master bedroom. The solution? Paint the furniture black. Although covering mahogany with paint would horrify fans of natural-wood finishes, painted

Extending the bedposts and adding pillows, mirrors, pretty window treatments, and a chandelier give the sleeping portion of the room an elegant and adult feel.

furniture has a past with a pedigree: As far back as the 1700s, furniture makers often used paint to mask the fact that several kinds of wood were combined in a single piece. In this modern bedroom, black paint unifies the different pieces of furniture and gives each piece a bolder look and more visual weight, anchoring the quietly neutral color scheme.

Painting good furniture can decrease its value, but in this case the risk is outweighed by the end result. Although the furniture is good-quality, it does not have the increasing value that antique pieces possess. (Painting antique furniture is generally discouraged because it will decrease the value significantly.)

To paint over varnished furniture, the *While You Were Out* team breaks up the slick surface so paint will adhere better. Sanding is the usual method, but a liquid sanding product is sometimes easier. After wiping the surface with a tack cloth, the team applies several thin coats of paint for a smooth, even surface. It's important to let each coat dry completely before applying the next one. Otherwise, the paint will not adhere.

For a touch of glamour and contrast, the bedside tables are treated to a silver finish, which repeats on the lamp bases and the drawer pulls. The freehand design on the headboard echoes the silver note.

---

**RIGHT AND OPPOSITE** Fringed and tasseled pillows on the bed and chairs invite the family members to curl up and linger. Repeating the chair fringe on the bed pillows helps tie the conversation area to the bed and gives that portion of the room a unified look.

## "I love juxtaposing opposite textures. It adds a layer of dimension, especially to monochromatic rooms." —*Ali Barone*

**Hanging Candle Holder**

1 Cut a piece of plywood for the base. Drill a hole through each corner the same diameter as the metal rod to be used to hang the shelf. Cut four threaded metal rods to the desired length, allowing enough length for the rods to go through the shelf and be screwed into a bolt. Attach the rod to the plywood with one bolt above the plywood and one below, to hold the structure together.

2 Cut PVC to fit over the threaded metal rods. Paint the shelf, PVC, and bolts black. Slip the PVC over the rods. Screw spring-release ceiling anchors, see *left*, onto the upper end of each rod. Suspend the shelf by drilling holes in the ceiling and fitting the anchors through the holes.

While a hanging candle shelf adds a touch of romance to the suite, its straight lines keep the look appropriate for homework and bill-paying sessions. Hanging the candles frees up the table below for a cup of coffee or a bowl of popcorn.

# Glazing Walls

1 To glaze the walls, combine latex paint with latex glazing medium to give the finish a more transparent look. This lets the color underneath show through and gives the walls a richer, deeper look because the paint is layered. Brush the paint-glaze mix onto the walls with a regular paintbrush. To get paint into the crevices of embossed wallpaper, use a small, stiff-bristle artist's brush.

2 While the glaze is still wet, wipe it away with a soft, lint-free rag. The finish should be uneven but blended. Occasionally stand back and look at the overall finish to check for areas that may be too light, or too dark, or splotchy. If the finish is too light, apply additional coats. To emphasize the embossing, let more paint stay in the crevices.

If in doubt, paint it black! Used correctly,
black can be a powerful statement or a
polite background that goes with everything.

## "...I just wanted to give [a gift] back to her for everything that she has done for me." —Lauren

### Enhance the Basics

Although the bed has great lines, it needed to make a stronger statement, so the *While You Were Out* team refashioned the corner posts. Extending them with turned posts and finials gives the bed the proportions of a traditional four-poster. Chayse emphasized the window at the head of the bed by adding gathered sheer panels and a pleated valance. These create an elegant backdrop for the painted headboard.

Chayse's design makes the bed a focal point so the different areas don't overwhelm the eye. A new duvet with a tone-on-tone scroll pattern and a sheer bed skirt bring the colors and textures of the window treatment into the room to reinforce the mood of quiet elegance. Fringed throw pillows and a purple-cased body pillow introduce a dollop of cool color to enliven the neutral scheme. (Notice how the purple fabric pulls out the color of the mountains in a nearby painting. Using a favorite piece of art as a source for color accents in the room calls more attention to the art and unifies a decorating scheme.) Elaborate Venetian-style mirrors with beveled scalloped edging flank the window and reflect both daylight and lamplight. Installing a chandelier near the foot of the bed completes the opulent look.

Cutting off the top of the computer hutch and turning it into a

**RIGHT** Turning the huge computer hutch into a desk helps it fit in with the bedroom furniture. Hanging a sheer curtain at the end of the desk creates a fabric wall that distinctly divides the work area from the sleeping and conversation areas.

## Upholstery Tips

When choosing upholstery, look for fabrics that are heavy enough to bear extensive handling and stapling yet still have enough give and stretch to go around curves and corners easily. Whenever possible, remove and save the original cover to use as a pattern. Pad the furniture frame with upholstery foam and top it with batting. Cut the fabric for a rough fit and lay it in place. Beginning at the center, stretch the fabric to one side and staple it in place. If possible, hide the staples underneath the piece or in a spot that can be covered with trim. Move to the opposite side and staple the cover in place directly across from the first staple. Continue working in this manner so the fabric remains taut but not distorted. Miter corners by folding the fabric and trimming any excess fabric. After the cover is in place, trim the excess margins close to the staples.

## Extending Bedposts

**1** The original short finials were cut from the bed using a straight, even cut. Longer posts were selected to match the size and proportion of the original finials. (Note: If necessary, the purchased posts can be shortened or several short ones can be stacked together. Experiment until you find the right combination.)

**2** Many purchased posts have an extension for adding a finial. If you select such a post, drill a matching hole in the original piece to receive the extension. If there is no extension, drill a hole in both pieces and use a wooden dowel to join them. Wood putty can fill in any gaps between the pieces so they will look like one solid piece.

## "In bedrooms people should address color and then evolve a plan from there—floors, walls, linens, lampshades, etcetera." —Chayse Dacoda

desk reduced its overbearing presence and helped integrate it with the other furniture.

Finally, to add architectural interest to plain walls, crown molding, a chair rail, and window cornices were added. The moldings frame and finish the room. The result is a unified space where the furnishings, accessories, windows, and walls work together to create a modern take on traditional style.

### Create a Place with a Purpose

To make the room as hardworking as it is beautiful, different areas were assigned specific tasks. A pair of slipper chairs and a small table provide a conversation spot. No more sitting on the floor as everyone gathers at the end of the day! The slipper chair fabric repeats the color of the bedding, and the custom-made metal table was painted black to visually connect the conversation corner and the sleeping area.

Pulling the workstation away from the bed and conversation spot creates an office-like extension to the room. To further define this area as a separate space, Chayse hung a drapery panel on a short, swing-arm rod.

For a final touch, a hanging shelf packed with stout pillar candles brings a bit of romance to the room. When other family members head their separate ways, Sandra and her husband can relax and enjoy their new Southern suite.

**LEFT** A golden lamp misted with silver spray-paint ties together the neutral color of the duvet with the silver end tables, picture frames, and chandelier. Beading on the lampshade adds sparkle that echoes the shine and shimmer of the mirror. To perk up a plain lampshade, glue trim to the lower edge, using hot glue or fabric glue.

# Big Dreams

Multipurpose rooms have big demands placed on them. See how the WYWO team transforms stressed-out spaces into functional and fantastic rooms.

# Miracle Myles

## and the Big, Beautiful Basement

## Six-year-old Myles has successfully battled a life-threatening tumor, but it cost his family their house. The WYWO team helps turn their basement rental into a new home.

Shawn, Barry, Megan, and Myles have spent the past few years facing a dreadful situation—the potential fatal illness of a family member. When Myles was diagnosed with an inoperable tumor, doctors gave the family little hope that the young boy would survive. Myles the Miracle survived and is thriving, but the family had to sell their home in order to pay for his medical treatment. Until they can get back on their feet, a large, open basement rental is home. Even though it's clean and comfortable, the basement lacks a homey feeling.

Shawn's sister Beverly called in the *While You Were Out* team to perform a miracle makeover. Because of the scope of the project and the challenges the family has faced, the budget was doubled, and extra help in the form of family and friends was called in. Designer John Bruce took on the challenge of turning a rather disjointed area into a unified space, using color, texture, and over 60 yards of fabric.

Host Evan Farmer and carpenters Leslie Segrete and Andrew Dan-Jumbo jump in to help with the huge space; so do plenty of family and friends. There's a lot to be accomplished in 48 hours: walls to cover, walls to build, sofas to re-cover and slipcover, gallons of paint to apply, and memories to create and preserve.

Stacked and spray-painted rattan spheres are fitted with light kits. The ceiling panel lights are also projects, created with papier-mâché. Other lamps in the room were prizes.

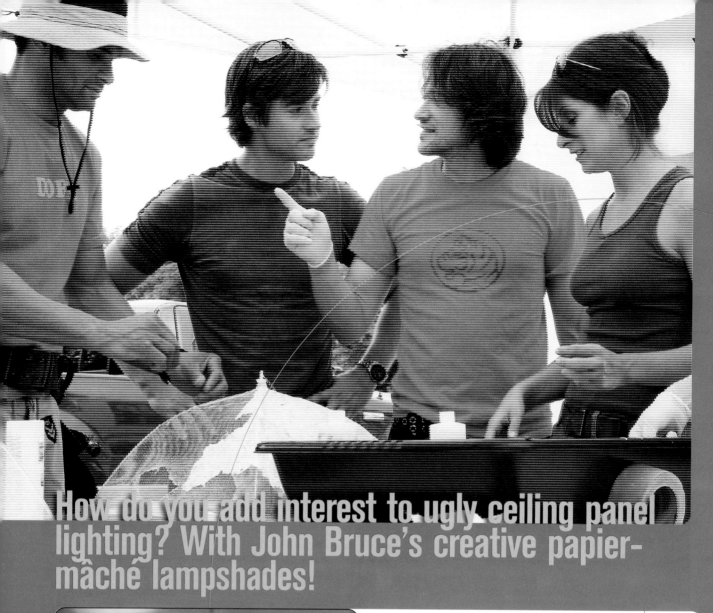

How do you add interest to ugly ceiling panel lighting? With John Bruce's creative papier-mâché lampshades!

### A Room for Myles

The first priority is carving out a room for Myles. The challenge is to provide the boy with his own space but not block light from his room or others. Walls made of frosted acrylic sheeting embedded with grass provide privacy but still let the light shine through *(see page 124)*. The family members can easily remove this type of structure and take it with them when they move. Butting the structure up against the basement walls and fitting it snugly between load-bearing supports means less construction and more stability.

### Clever Cover-Ups

The basement walls had a cold and institutional look. Making matters worse, the building materials used varied from one wall to the next. Because the walls were different, John designed several solutions for hiding the problem surfaces and unsightly areas of the room. Although the treatments varied, he created

**LEFT** Leslie covered this sofa in family-friendly fabric and made matching pillows to add comfort to the back. **OPPOSITE** Shaggy rugs provide welcome texture in the basement space. This one drapes a seating bench for the kids; other rugs define living zones in the open floor plan.

# Acrylic Room Dividers

1 Measure the opening where the room divider will be installed. Make a ½x2-inch board framework to fit these measurements. (Note: 2-inch side of the board is the frame depth.) Measure the inner dimensions of the framework. Use the measurements to cut ½x1-inch boards for an inner frame, mitering the 1-inch-wide corners.

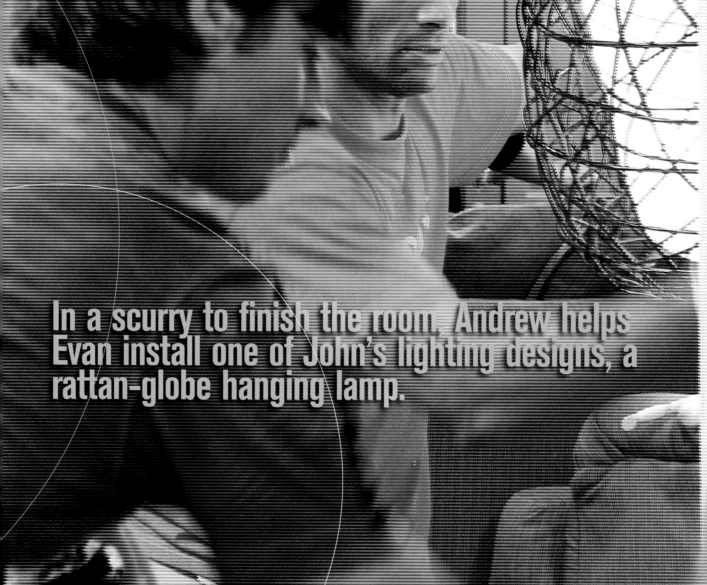

In a scurry to finish the room, Andrew helps Evan install one of John's lighting designs, a rattan-globe hanging lamp.

**2** Glue and screw the mitered corners. Screw the inner frame to the outer frame (the narrow side of inner frame boards should be perpendicular to the outer frame boards; screw through the outer frame into the inner frame boards to attach). Countersink the screws and fill the holes with wood putty. Stain or paint the boards, if desired, at this stage.

**3** Following the manufacturer's directions, trim the acrylic sheet to fit into the opening. Rest the acrylic sheet on the inner frame. Create a second inner frame and place it on top of the acrylic sheet (the two inner frames should sandwich the acrylic sheet). Screw the frame in place. Install the frame in the opening; the fit should be snug so that no mounting hardware is needed.

Before

Before

MIRACLE MYLES

Sewing Pillows

## "They've been through a tough experience...I wanted the space to be more comfortable." —Beverly

continuity by choosing a neutral color palette for the surface treatments and fabrics. Textural and pattern changes add interest and warmth to the space.

To warm up the cinder-block walls, Andrew fastened boards horizontally. A ¼-inch gap between the boards gives the walls depth and interest and lets a bit of color show through. To support the strips, Andrew attached vertical studs to the walls every three feet.

Other walls and some corners were covered with fabric. Some treatments, made to look like drapes, were hung on drapery or tension rods. Additional cover-ups were devised using sheets of heavy fabric the team adhered to the walls with heavy-duty hook-and-loop tape.

### Divide and Conquer

Dividing the wide-open space into smaller units makes the room feel more intimate and user-friendly. The acrylic panels used for Myles' room were one method John implemented to segment the space. The panels provide privacy yet do not block the flow of light.

Another solution is a book and storage shelf he used to separate the living and dining areas. To make the back of the shelf appear more like a wall and less like the back of a storage unit, family photographs were put in identical wooden frames and hung in a grid. Keeping the frames uniform in size and very plain places the emphasis on the photographs.

Furniture and area rugs also help define the individual spaces and identify their specific purpose. Sofas and chairs clustered together indicate an area for visiting or TV viewing. Rugs establish boundaries at floor level and direct traffic through the space.

**OPPOSITE John's design plan included a book for Myles that documented the makeover process. The sketch shows John's idea for a lamp that he crafted for Myles' new bedroom. RIGHT The multifunctional room is now a peaceful place to relax and consider the future.**

1 Cut a square, rectangle, or round shape from kraft paper to make a pattern. Place the pattern on the fabric, aligning it with the grain. Cut out two pieces (allow an extra ½ inch around the edges for a seam). Place the two pieces of fabric, right sides together, and pin along the perimeter. Sew the two pieces together, leaving a 6-inch opening at the bottom.

2 Clip the corners of the pillow if it's a square or rectangle; clip every inch or so if it's round. Turn the pillow right side out. Carefully poke into the corners so the pillow has a nice shape. Stuff the pillow with polyester fiberfill until it is full. Pin the opening closed, tucking the extra seam allowance inside. Slip-stitch the opening closed.

## Ceiling Tile Lampshades

**1** Pour fabric stiffener into a plastic dishpan. Tear heavy-weight rag paper into strips approximately 3 inches wide and dip them one at a time into the stiffener. When the paper is saturated, carefully pull a strip from the liquid and drape it over a wire fly net (traditionally used to protect pies or fruit). Continue doing this until the entire form is covered with about a ⅛-inch layer of paper.

**2** Set the fly-net form aside. When the paper is nearly dry, slip the form out and set the lampshade aside to let the papier-mâché finish drying. When the shade is dry, fit the new lampshade over the existing light cover. If desired, trim the edges with narrow picture-frame molding, mitering and gluing the corners. (Attach to the acrylic light-cover panel with screws to allow access to the light.)

## Paint, fabric, flooring, and wall materials in a neutral color palette make it easier to unify the space.

### Pull It Together

The family's furniture looked fine in the separate rooms of their old house, but thrown together into one large space, it resembled a hodgepodge. John chose to use color and pattern to solve the problem. By slipcovering the sofas and using pillows in coordinating colors and patterns, the *While You Were Out* team pulls the furniture together for a more unified look.

Repeating the wooden slat wall treatment also unites the different areas of the room. Paint and fabric get into the act as well. Sticking to a neutral color palette helps blend elements in the multipurpose space. Paint is used wherever possible; it's inexpensive, goes on quickly, and it adds cohesion to the design. Curtains shirred on rods hide closets and storage areas and dress the windows and French doors.

### Take It Away

Because this is temporary housing for the family, the shelving unit and accessory pieces are designed to be easily removed and repurposed in a variety of future spaces. Room-defining rugs roll up and move on to the next place. And because the furniture now blends, it will be a breeze to mix and match it in a new home. Even the fabric panels can be stripped from the walls and the draperies removed from the windows. The large pieces of fabric are enough yardage for refashioned window treatments, pillows, or slipcovers.

**OPPOSITE A wall of family photos makes this temporary space feel like home. A variety of lamps illuminates vignettes and encourages an intimate, more relaxed environment. RIGHT To cover countless wall problems, John used various treatments, including fabric draperies and horizontal oak planks.**

# Shades of Water

## Olympic swimmer Nate Dusing scores low marks with his boring living/dining room. He hopes to win points with a fabulous makeover to surprise his girlfriend.

turning a bland Austin, Texas, living space into a beautiful haven in less than two days on a tight budget was an Olympic-size task for designer Chayse Dacoda, host Evan Farmer, and carpenters Ali Barone and Jason Cameron. Together they teamed up with homeowner Nate Dusing, a medal-winning Olympic swimmer, who wanted help in creating a welcoming, multifunctional space for the love of his life, girlfriend Michelle.

Before

With Michelle hours away on a tour of Corpus Christi, the *While You Were Out* team got down to business. Chayse began the transformation with a well-thought-out design supported by several drawings, a floor plan, fabric swatches, and paint cards. Inspired by Nate's athletic focus, her primary design goal was to give the room "a feeling of water in all its forms." Her plan also included establishing continuity through clean-lined design.

### Color Cues

This large multipurpose space has an open floor plan that incorporates the kitchen, the dining table, and a seating area. With no architectural break such as a doorway or trim molding, the space seemed resigned to wearing a single neutral shade of paint, a common solution used in new homes with open floor plans.

But Chayse wanted to jazz the space with more than one color. Her goal to give the room "the feeling of reflecting water" spurred her decision to select three shades of paint, all in the same intensity. Each wall was painted a different color: pale green, light green, and pale aqua. Because the colors are closely related, the change from one to another is subtle but effectively gives the space the right amount of spunk.

The selection of greens and blues, all equally weighted cool tones, connects the spaces to one another. The trio are also a suitable backdrop for the water theme Chayse wanted to establish. But while painting a room is one of the easiest and least expensive ways to add impact, finding the right colors and intensities can be challenging.

To evaluate wall color for a room, professionals suggest painting sample boards in

This large space, a living/dining room combo, was painted with a different color on each wall. Keeping the wall colors close in intensity made the result visually interesting yet peaceful.

# Bench Seat

1 This bench can be created in various widths and lengths to suit the space available. (Benches longer than 5 feet will need additional legs in the center.) Start by making a frame of 1×4-inch boards in the dimensions desired. Create a ledge on the inside of the frame by lining it with 1×3-inch boards screwed into the outer frame.

**2** Use 4×4-inch posts or two 2×4s butted and screwed together at a right angle for the legs (leg length depends on personal preferences). Bolt the legs to the inner corners of the frame. Sand the entire piece, using medium-grit sandpaper followed by fine-grit sandpaper. Wipe with a tack cloth. Stain and clear-coat, or paint, the piece following the manufacturer's directions.

**3** Cut a piece of ½-inch plywood or MDF (medium-density fiberboard) to fit inside the frame. Cover the piece with fabric, stapling the fabric to the underside. Rest the upholstered plywood on the bench's inner ledge. Make two box pillows to fit the bench seat, using 4-inch-thick foam cut to size. Cover the foam with upholstery fabric.

The new lounge area is a calm and inviting space for watching television or conversing with friends and family. Dark woods ground the leggier pieces so they balance against the heavy sofas.

## Fishbowl Table

**1** Begin with a ready-made coffee table and a fishbowl. Measure for and mark the center of the coffee table, or place the bowl off-center if desired. Measure the fishbowl at its widest diameter. Subtract at least ½ inch from this measurement for an opening that will allow the bowl to be suspended (holes cut larger may cause the bowl to fall through).

**2** Mark the circle opening using a compass or the pencil-and-string method. Mask around the circle with painter's or masking tape to reduce surface splintering. Drill a hole into the surface; then insert the jigsaw blade and cut out the circle. Sand the opening until smooth; wipe with a tack cloth. Stain and clear-coat or paint the opening to match the tabletop. Insert the bowl.

# "Our finished rooms don't have a billion tchotchkes...Everything is in an appropriate location..." – *Evan Farmer*

the colors to be tested. It's wise to use boards with a texture similar to the walls that will be painted, because texture affects the appearance of the color. Paint looks darker on rough surfaces than on smooth ones. If textured boards aren't available, it's a good idea to add texture to the foam-core boards to mimic the walls.

When WYWO designers choose the paint sheen, or finish, that's best for the room, they keep in mind that the shinier the paint, the lighter the color will appear. Gloss and semigloss paints will emphasize any defects in the wall surface, however, so they're best for smooth surfaces and woodwork. Eggshell finish has a subtle sheen that gives the color more depth than a flat finish.

Many designers advise painting boards with the colors under consideration and then moving the sample boards around the room to see how they look at different times of the day and evening and to note how the color changes with the light. This also lets you evaluate how the paint colors interact with other items in the room, such as upholstery, artwork, and flooring.

## Intimate Areas

To make the large, undivided space more functional and welcoming, Chayse arranged the furniture to define specific areas: Clustering seating pieces in a tight U shape on one side of the room creates a cozy conversation area. The dining table and chairs are placed on the other side of the room to define the dining area. A large area rug grounds the seating group, which turns its back on the dining area to focus on the television and a wall of art. In large rooms, placing the sofa in the center creates a psychological wall that directs traffic around instead of through the seating area.

To contain the electronics and the television, Jason built a

---

OPPOSITE **The bench is a sleek addition to the room and provides additional seating.** RIGHT **The coffee table now has a resident goldfish. If the fish moves to a new home, the bowl can be filled with a collection of seashells or a few small plants.**

# "I want to thank her for being with me while I trained for the Olympics." *—Nate Dusing*

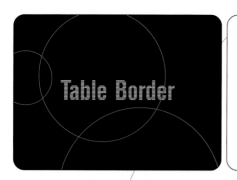

## Table Border

**1** Bordering a ready-made table is a way to add drama to an otherwise boring piece of furniture. Because tabletop thickness and fabrication methods vary, begin by studying how your table is made. If no supports will be damaged, prepare the outer perimeter of the table by routing the outer edge to receive a metal T-strip trim piece (used for floor transitions).

## "I like to blend things that contradict: linear pieces with ethnic...wood with metal. With each layer, you notice more." – *Chayse Dacoda*

component wall unit. This is a perfect solution for those who are in temporary quarters or for those still acquiring quality furniture. The pieces are inexpensive to make and can be reconfigured and broken apart to fit into a variety of spaces.

To further define the dining room, Chayse installed a chandelier over the table. This marks the area as a place apart from the rest of the room, and a dimmer switch offers the opportunity for more intimacy. To get the look of a high-end light fixture, Chayse and Nate transformed the inexpensive brass chandelier by preparing the metal with a primer and then ragging on silver paint. The aged finish works well with the cool blues in the room.

Chayse also remade the dining table to give it more presence and character. To the original light-wood table, she added a border of dark-stained boards accented with a narrow strip in a putty color. The boards are butted tightly against the edge of the tabletop, and a connector piece, screwed to the underside of the tabletop provides extra support.

### Accent with Personality

Nate's passion for the water inspired the choice of accessories in the room. For example, Nate's coffee table was reworked to hold a fishbowl. A reflecting pool, using another bowl, was created on the second shelf of the television unit. The bowl is lit from below, to cast soft, watery reflections onto the walls above. Wall plaques featuring water-theme photos hang as a mass grouping above the television unit.

### Keep It Simple

The furniture in the room consists of a few important pieces with simple, modern lines. The tables and shelving unit are understated and clean looking. For extra seating, Chayse designed a classic bench with white faux-suede cushions. The room is simple and elegant, proving once again high style doesn't have to be costly.

---

**LEFT** Bordering a plain table is a fast way to give it a custom look. **OPPOSITE** The dining area gains importance with a dressed-up table and new, darker-tone chairs. The poster on the wall was framed with molding found at a home-improvement center.

**2** Measure the table and cut the T-strip pieces to fit each side, mitering the corners. Cut the outer wood border to fit the perimeter of the table, mitering the corners. Rout the inner edge of the borders to fit into the T-strip. Sand, stain, and apply polyurethane finish to the border pieces, according to the manufacturer's directions. Glue and screw the T-strips to the table edge.

**3** Mount a support piece of ¼-inch to ½-inch plywood under the table's outer edge, so that it extends enough to support the border. Glue the prefinished border pieces to the T-strip and screw through the support from underneath to secure (check screw length first). Use additional screws underneath the table, on each side of the mitered corners, to hold them tightly together.

# Cloud Nine Kitchen

## Chrystalyn and Marla have told their mother, Sandra, that she is their inspiration. To show their appreciation they want to give her dated green kitchen a modern look.

for years Sandra has dreamed of a clean, white kitchen complete with white cabinets and chrome hardware. But expanses of green flooring and countertop, expensive to replace, have kept her kitchen redo at the dream stage. A hanging lamp straight from the '70s, dark wood cabinets and furniture, and wallpaper with a small print add to the dated look. Andrew Dan-Jumbo, Leslie Segrete, and host Evan Farmer all agree—this look is well past its prime.

Sandra, her daughters say, is a true example of giving, sacrifice, and helping others find the right path. So designer John Bruce planned a "cloud nine" kitchen for this angel of mercy, working blue into the white background and punching it with bright orange. Molded plastic pedestal chairs with a '60s look and a hanging light made from PVC pipe bring a hip retro vibe into the room.

*Before*

A half-wall between the kitchen and living space was a precarious perch for the television. John had to come up with a way to integrate the television into the design so it would be an asset instead of an eyesore.

### Kitchen Fresh

Removing the extensive amounts of green and brown instantly updates the room. The process requires patience and elbow grease, but the results are worth it. The doors come off the kitchen cabinets, and the varnish is stripped with a chemical stripper, wire brush, and scraper. The cabinet frames get a good sanding to remove the varnish and dark color. Once stripped, the cabinets receive a whitewash treatment with a white stain specifically made for whitewashing. After the first coat dries, the process is repeated until the desired color and opaqueness are achieved. When the cabinets are as light as John wants them, they're sealed with a clear sealer. This treatment allows the wood grain to show through, creating a warmer look than you would get with an opaque finish that hides the grain and mimics laminate or veneer. The whitewashed wood grain also blends with the new wood floor. Shiny silver hinges and chrome handles complete the cabinet facelift.

Soft blue and white take this kitchen, a child of the '70s, into the future. Splashes of orange, a fun light fixture, and designer-style chairs create a fresh retro look.

# Modern Chandelier

**1** PVC pipe cut at different lengths and angles and placed in two concentric rows forms the base for a Scandinavian-inspired chandelier. Start with a clear acrylic tube that is fitted with a shade fixture at the top (a purchased clear lamp could be substituted). Cut the PVC pipe longer than the acrylic tube, cutting the inner row at 45-degree angles and the outer row at 60-degree angles.

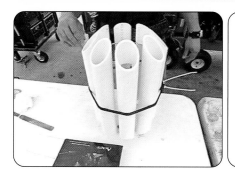

2 Line up the inner set of pipes and hold them in place with a bungee cord. Using dots of epoxy, glue the pipes in place. After the glue dries, remove the bungee cord and put the second row of pipes in place. Glue the second row to the first one and hold it in place with a bungee cord until it dries. Use a purchased hanging lamp kit to wire the lamp, then hang it from the ceiling.

# The lighter wood opens up the kitchen and gives it a whole new attitude.

*While You Were Out* designers and carpenters have found that new hardware doesn't always match up with the holes left behind by old cupboard handles and drawer pulls. They solve the problem by filling in the old holes with a dowel of the same diameter, cut to match the thickness of the cupboard or drawer front. The dowel is pounded into the hole using a rubber mallet and held with wood glue. They finish the repair with paintable wood putty, sand it smooth, and then paint the cupboard or drawer. When the paint is dry, they drill new holes and install the new hardware.

## Smart Surfaces

A hardwood floor that floats over existing flooring makes the green vinyl disappear in short order. The lighter wood opens up the kitchen and gives it a whole new attitude. "Floating" hardwood floors install over an existing floor as long as the original is level and even. They are cheaper and easier to install than traditional wood floors, and there is less chance of warping because the design of the material allows for only a small amount of expansion and shrinkage.

The green countertop is next to go: a new white one takes its place. Gypsum with a wavy pattern covers up the half-wall between the kitchen and living space, adding texture to the divider. John painted the original dark wood table white, and Andrew cut a piece of acrylic countertop material to fit the top. Its turned legs say traditional style, but its clean white color links it to the 1960s chairs.

## Got the Blues

Instead of stripping the wallpaper, the team paints over it with a soft blue hue. Although some designers disagree, others insist that it's fine to paint over wallpaper if you prepare the surface properly first. The wallpaper must fit tightly against the wall and

**OPPOSITE A painted "branch," sprouting wires and alligator clips, sits on the half-wall to hold notes and memos, keeping the refrigerator and counters uncluttered. RIGHT Sleek plastic pedestal chairs with burnt orange cushions are fashioned after those popular in the '60s.**

have no bubbles or loose seams. If it is vinyl-coated, sand it lightly to roughen the surface so paint will adhere. Wash it down to remove any residue or dirt, even if sanding wasn't required. When the surface dries, roll on one or two coats of opaque primer; then apply one or two coats of color.

The backsplash got a case of the blues too. Blue vinyl sheeting was glued between the countertops and the cabinetry with contact cement; the vinyl is washable and provides interesting texture in the room. Even the switchplates are covered, so they don't detract from the clean look.

## Lighten Up

For a hanging light that looks as if it came from the days of mod, PVC pipe is cut at different lengths and angles and glued around a clear acrylic cylinder in two concentric rows. Epoxy holds it all together. The trick is to keep the parts from shifting while the epoxy dries. A bungee cord wrapped around the center keeps the pieces in place while dabs of epoxy are slipped between the PVC and the cylinder. Once the first row is secure, the second one is applied in the same way.

For a fun countertop light with a soft, sweet glow, real sugar cubes are hot-glued into a cylindrical shape. A purchased lamp base provides the soft light. Display-style lighted bases like this can be found at gifts and crafts stores.

## Good Viewing

To make the television blend in with the rest of the kitchen, John designed shelving units for the end of the room divider. Half circles and quarter circles extend from just above the floor to well above the ledge. Chrome legs hold it all together and match the new drawer and cupboard handles. The curves of the shelf are in tune with the rounded shapes of the new light fixtures, chairs, and table, so the shelves look like part of the original design instead of an add-on.

---

**LEFT** Textured vinyl brings color to the backsplash and makes cleanup a snap. **OPPOSITE** Gleaming pots, pans, and kitchen utensils match the chrome hinges and handles on the cabinets. The hinges were spray-painted to match the rest of the metals.

"…We just wanted to reward her for her faithfulness. We love her!" *—Chrystalyn and Marla*

# "John Bruce is the master of finding new and unusual materials" like the molded gypsum for the room divider.—*Andrew Dan-Jumbo*

The television sits on a lazy Susan, so it can be turned to face either room. Swivel bases designed for televisions are available at home centers and home-furnishings stores. A floating shelf above the TV takes the eye higher so the black screen becomes less noticeable and dominating.

## Orange Punch

The blue and white palette is pleasant, but orange art glass and chair cushions give it real pizzazz. This blast of complementary color draws the eye into the room and energizes the cool colors with a dose of their opposites on the color wheel. Pairing contrasting colors makes each member more intense and more interesting; it's a no-fail way to create a pleasing color scheme.

For a twist on a traditional notepad or chalk board, John devised a pair of orange and white topiaries planted in plaster-filled pots. Wires and alligator clips sprout from the tops to hold family memos, recipes, or even mementos. When placed on the room divider, they become functional sculptures.

## Living Large

A living area opens up beyond the kitchen half-wall, extending the space the family has for relaxing and congregating. Now

---

**OPPOSITE** This gypsum board has a molded wavy texture and adds interest to the room divider. The curved shelves on the end add style and function. **RIGHT** The orange art glass, a prize, sparks the room with complementary color.

Room Divider Shelving

1 Cut four half-circle shelves and two quarter-circle shelves from MDF (medium-density fiberboard). Sand the shelves and wipe with a tack cloth. Prime and paint the shelves, following the manufacturer's directions. Use threaded rods covered with metal tubes and PVC pipes to support the shelves. (Note: The height of the shelf supports will vary; cut supports to suit the installation.)

2 Mark and drill holes for the threaded rod/shelf supports in the shelves. Screw the bottom half-circle shelf to the top of the half-wall. Screw in the threaded rods/shelf supports. Build a U-shape frame to separate and support the two upper half-circle shelves; construct the shelf. Mount a smaller U-shape frame to the wall studs, see *left*. Slip the shelf over the frame and screw it in place at the sides.

**Pickling Cabinets**

**1** Remove the doors, drawers, and any other components from the kitchen cabinets. Also remove the hardware and set it aside. Following the directions exactly, apply commercial chemical stripper to remove the varnish and stain. Wear safety goggles, gloves, and any other recommended protective gear. For small grooves and crevices, use a wire brush. Sand the base cabinets.

**2** After all the components are stripped, sand the pieces and wipe them clean with a tack cloth. Following the manufacturer's instructions, apply a white stain that's specifically intended for whitewashed or pickled effects. (Check with home-improvement centers or paint stores for this type of stain.) Let dry. Finish the cabinets with a coat of polyurethane.

# Pickling washes color over the grain to reduce contrast, thus bringing out the rich textures of the wood.

that the kitchen has been redone, a few extra touches will help the two areas flow together as one unified space. One way to do this is to frame several pieces of artwork in the same manner and hang them together for maximum impact. Here, leftover scraps of the textured gypsum board make quick and easy picture frames for artwork hung in the living room, *left*.

To create frames like this, select the artwork or photographs to be framed, then determine how large the frame should be to create the best effect. A frame with borders slightly wider than the height of the image, such as the one shown *left*, will accent a small piece of art and give it more visual power than a narrow frame. The wide frame takes the place of a combined frame and mat but has a sleeker look.

John made the frames by cutting gypsum to the desired outer dimensions, then cutting a hole for the artwork in the center. Two coats of paint blend the gypsum into the room's color scheme. He then centered the artwork on the back side of the gypsum and secured it with archival-quality picture tape. Brown kraft paper covers the entire back of the frame to protect both the art and the wall. To ensure that the paper backing fits tightly, he glues it in place, then lightly spritzes it with water to shrink the paper. With a picture hanger secured carefully to the upper back of the frame, the art is ready to hang.

**LEFT Scraps of textured gypsum board form frames that cost virtually nothing. Look for inexpensive art in the form of postcards, pretty ribbons woven together, small prints or posters, favorite photographs, or projects made by family members.**

# Day Dreams

Active living spaces get star treatment from the *While You Were Out* team. See how changing these rooms can bring a fantasy to life.

# Montano's Mystery

## Colleen and Allison are a rare pair: roommates who have never had a fight. To celebrate, Colleen wants to surprise Allison with a patio turned Parisian bistro.

**a**llison isn't the only one in for a surprise in this episode. Instead of the usual three weeks, designer Mark Montano will have less than one day to do his planning and design, and the team will buy all their materials that same day. The biggest surprise, though, is that Mark doesn't know he'll be doing an outdoor room—something he's never done before.

The "courtyard" of Colleen and Allison's townhouse is a barebones brick patio surrounded by a few scrub plantings and a tall wooden fence. Colleen's dream is to turn it into something that will reflect the Parisian vacation that Allison endlessly talks about.

The small space presents a challenge with its lack of shade, minimal plantings, unsightly air-conditioning unit, and lack of lighting. Fortunately it has loads of character. The narrow space and brick patio already have the feel of an outdoor cafe that you might find along a Paris side street. There's even a miniature Eiffel Tower garden sculpture hidden behind some of the plants. Mark uses this as his inspiration (and uses the sculpture as a table centerpiece, *opposite*).

### Parisian Patio
A light whitewash on the wooden fence enhances the rustic European look of the finished design and makes the space feel airy

Happy colors and fresh fabrics grace this patio and give it a country-French aesthetic. The linens, seat slipcovers, and pillows are easy-care and washable.

"Working with the people on the show has helped me to see that there are even more possibilities...I love to collaborate..." – *Mark Montano*

and open. Most of the plantings are plucked out of the perimeter of the little yard to reduce visual clutter and expand the space visually. Landscaping tarp covers the ground to discourage weeds, and a covering of crushed brick covers the tarp to create a more urban feeling. Containers full of plants can be placed on the crushed brick. Growing flowers, herbs, and even vegetables is in keeping with the French theme, and the pots can be moved around if guests need standing room.

To disguise the air-conditioning unit, the team builds a small fencelike structure that is open on the top and the back. Space between the slats allows for good airflow to the air-conditioner, and the box lifts off easily when the unit needs maintenance.

The patio will be used primarily for entertaining, so a community table is the key piece of furniture. Porch posts form the shapely legs for the $2\frac{1}{2}\times4$-foot table. Using a T-shape base leaves plenty of room under the table so the benches can slide beneath it when the table is not in use. Stowing the benches

**LEFT** A candle chandelier was created from two inverted wire shelves. **OPPOSITE** Foam cushions cut to fit the tops of the picnic table stools are covered with fabric that is pinned and stitched at the corners. A ruffle finishes the lower edge of each cushion to complete the cafe look.

# Candle Chandelier

**1** Select two identical, ready-made wire shelves with flat backs and half-circle fronts. The shelves used for this project have scrollwork brackets; when the shelves are turned upside down, the brackets become the top of the fixture. Place the two shelves back-to-back and wire them together in several places using needle-nose pliers to twist the wires tightly. Clip the wires and bend under.

**2** Hang the chandelier from a white chain wired to the brackets. (Note: If desired, the chain and chandelier can be spray-painted at this point.) Create a wire collar for candle jars. To suspend the cups from the chandelier, attach three lengths of wire to each collar and twist them together to make a hanger. Hang the cups equal distances from one another, so the chandelier is balanced.

## "Mark Montano designs happiness. Period. I love working with Mark because he's an emotionally committed designer." – *Evan Farmer*

under the table opens up more space for walking and mingling. A plank tabletop on the picnic table stays in keeping with the rustic feel of the bricks and wooden fence and will have character and interest when the table is bare of linens. The four 18×16½-inch benches are constructed of similar materials, but an X design was used for the legs to add stability (see *page 154* for how-to instructions).

A small round bistro table and folding chairs offer more intimate seating in another part of the patio. The little table is perfect for coffee and breakfast in the morning or as a buffet for a dinner or cocktail party. It can also be folded up and stashed behind the fence if more mingling space is needed.

For late-night dining, Mark created new exterior lights to install on the patio. Hanging lights constructed from dome-shape wire hanging baskets are placed at strategic points for illumination and ambience. To create the lights, Mark removed the moss lining from vinyl-coated wire baskets. An exterior light socket is inserted through the bottom of one basket and a light bulb screwed in place. A second basket is then aligned rim to

---

**ABOVE, LEFT** Fabric coordinates include a plaid and a toile design. **RIGHT** Mark sketched this elevation in his hotel room the night before the makeover. **OPPOSITE** The finished patio is a pleasant retreat with French country charm.

## Bench

**1** Use two staircase balusters for each crossed leg. Locate the place where the two legs will cross; drill a ½-inch-diameter hole through each leg at that spot. Insert a ½-inch dowel through both balusters to connect them. Mark and cut the bottom of the legs at an angle so they sit squarely on the floor. Attach the base of the legs to a support board with screws (see photo at *left*).

**2** Flip the bench over and measure the inner rectangle created by the legs. Build an open-box framework from 2×2-inch boards (this box connects to the legs at each outer corner and is the platform for the seat). Use plywood or MDF (medium-density fiberboard) for the seat. Drill up through the box with a countersink bit and use wood screws to attach the seat to the box framework.

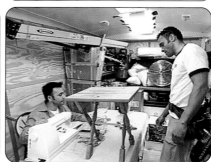

rim and wired to the first. These wire globes hang as accent lights. For the focal-point lighting over the table, Mark fashioned a chandelier from two half-round wire wall shelves turned upside down (so the scrollwork brackets become the chandelier top). Wire joins the two shelves and also holds the glass votive cups and tea lights that dangle from the chandelier, providing the romance of candlelight. A hanging chain is added to the top and voilà!—instant elegance (see *page 151* for instructions).

### Weather-Worthy

A fabric awning will give shelter from the sun and rain. Three curve-top trellises form the structure that will hold up the awning fabric. The trellises are bolted to the fence, and the fabric is draped over the top and stapled in place so it won't blow away. The trellises also support the globe-shape lights.

Thick cushions with flirty skirts soften the seating on each bench. The slipcovers fit tightly over the foam cushion, like a shower cap, but the cushions aren't attached to the benches. If

**LEFT** Purchased dishware was awarded as a prize. **OPPOSITE** Mark's special challenge was to design this outdoor space after arriving at the site. To quickly establish his color palette and French country look, he selected readily available fabric coordinates that unify the space.

"She's an incredible roommate...I couldn't think of a better way to surprise her..." – *Colleen*

Before

Before

Old-World Art

1 Cut a large free-form shape from MDF (medium density fiberboard); see photo, *opposite*. Paint the back with exterior paint to weather-seal the board; let dry. Mount the board to the wall using the appropriate hardware. Mask around the form and protect the wall surface with plastic sheeting. Roll textured paint onto the board and cut edges with a high-nap roller; let dry.

2 Crumple a reproduction poster and dip it into coffee. Brush decoupage medium onto the board and glue the wet poster to the board, tearing the edges in places. Age the poster and board by brushing on diluted dark brown paint over the entire surface. Apply another coat of decoupage medium. Let dry. Seal the board with two coats of weatherproof polyurethane.

# The little table is perfect for coffee and breakfast in the mornings, or as a buffet for a dinner or cocktail party.

inclement weather is on the horizon, it's easy to gather up the cushions and bring them indoors. (Although these cushion covers were made from ordinary upholstery fabric, weatherproof acrylic fabrics could also be used.)

Because all the light fixtures are made from vinyl-coated wire units and hung with vinyl-coated chain, there's no need to worry about rust. Also, using vinyl-coated wire to join the pieces that make up the fixtures prevents rust stains developing as the pieces weather the elements.

## Ooh La La

To add an aged look to the patio area, Mark applied a faux-stucco technique to the brick wall. MDF cut in irregular shapes is screwed into the brick, then coated with yellow textured paint. Inexpensive reproduction French posters are aged by crumpling and soaking briefly in diluted coffee. While still wet, they are torn and further distressed, then decoupaged in layers over the faux stucco. They instantly take on the look of handbills that are past their prime.

Blue and yellow French-inspired patterns give the table linens a true bistro look. White geraniums hang from wire baskets attached to the fence and hint at the apartment window boxes that line the streets of Paris. Lush ivy, artificial for now, meanders along the wall. The mini Eiffel Tower that provided Mark's initial inspiration takes its proper place as a centerpiece. A simple wooden frame made to slip over the top and rest near the base can support squatty candles, turning a garden ornament into a candelabrum.

**OPPOSITE** Table linens and pillows add color and softness to the patio. Coordinates like these are available in the home-decorating section of fabric stores. **RIGHT** This old-world treatment is bolted to the wall for easy removal.

# Global Rhythm Garage

## The WYWO team drums up some ethnic style when Janice asks its members to convert an old stone garage into a music studio for her husband and daughter.

anice's husband, Ernie, dreams about learning to play the conga drums. Their daughter, Claudia, is already quite impressive on the drums. The family fantasy is to set up a father-daughter music room. Janice has the perfect solution: An unused stone garage behind the house could be the ideal place for musicians to jam. But how do you turn a garage into a music room that's also fit for entertaining other musicians and a possible audience?

Mark Montano came up with a bold design that he dubbed "global rhythm garage." Leslie Segrete, Andrew Dan-Jumbo, host Evan Farmer, and Janice are all in tune with Mark's plan. Playing up the stone and rustic wood walls, Mark chooses a variety of natural materials for floor, ceiling, and accessories. These items have an exotic feel in keeping with the global ethnic theme.

Before

A room full of natural and neutral materials can be boring if it lacks a focal point. Mark fends off boredom with a giant cutout in the shape of a tribal mask. Graphic shapes on pillows, wall hangings, and a bench add to the visual interest.

For a final touch, punches of red and yellow turn the design up a notch or two. They appear often enough to draw the eye around the room and create a sense of rhythm. When used too sparingly, bright jolts of color can be a visual distraction rather than a unifying asset.

### Creating Ambience

The rugged stone on the lower walls and the rustic wood above it give the garage character that could be molded into looks ranging from cottage chic to classic country to tribal ethnic. Elephant grass stapled to the open ceiling beams steers the space toward African design—a perfect match for a future conga drum player. The fire-resistant elephant grass comes stitched along one edge like the waistband of a hula skirt. To create the thatched effect, the banding is stapled to the ceiling along the center beam; additional staples secure the grass to the exposed roof beams, creating the look

Designs inspired by Kuba cloth are featured on the pillows, the wall hangings, and the sisal rug. The rustic bench, a challenging project, was made by carpenter Andrew Dan-Jumbo.

of a grass hut. If elephant grass is not readily available, look for other types of materials that drape well and have an ethnic appeal. Long strands of wooden beads or shells are available at some import stores. Textural fabrics such as burlap, grass cloth, and seed cloth (available at garden centers) would also work well as ceiling and wall covers.

On the floor, a sisal rug with hand-painted designs brings the texture full circle. Look for inexpensive sisal or jute rugs online and in import stores. Some come in typical room sizes, while others are configured in blocks that can be cut apart and rearranged to fit your space. Sisal-wrapped drum tables are right at home with the texture and the music.

### Keen on Kuba

The southeastern region of the Congo is home to the Kuba tribe, which is renowned for its graphic artwork. Highly collectible Kuba textiles feature a background woven from raffia and decorated with bold designs that are either woven into the background or added using appliqué or reverse appliqué. To mimic the pricey Kuba cloth for pillows and two giant wall hangings, Mark used faux suede and cut out bold graphic designs, which he then appliquéd to a plain fabric background. To find similar design inspirations, go online or to import stores and look for mud cloths

**LEFT** A large tribal mask framed in elephant grass announces the room's theme to all who enter. The ethnic look is a perfect match for the hutlike stone garage. **OPPOSITE** Simple furniture, rich textures, and graphic patterns carry out the tribal theme.

Designer Mark Montano adds interest to this monochromatic color scheme with a giant cutout in the shape of a tribal mask.

## Tribal-Inspired Bench

1 A bench constructed of 1×12 boards sports curves that echo the lines of the conga drums. Use two boards for the slatted seat and another pair for the back. Cut gentle curves for the leg pieces. Drill and cut openings in the back pieces to create the decorative pattern. Note the angle of the bottom edge of the back piece *below*. This angle allows the back to slant for more comfortable support.

2 After all the pieces are ready for assembly, join them with screws. Use a countersink drill bit to make a small hole for the screw and a larger opening above it. Cut sections of dowel to fit the larger hole; they'll act as plugs that cover the screws. This will give the impression that the bench was joined by pegs. Rub the bench with dark stain, wiping away any excess color.

or Kuba cloths. Mud cloths, which are also highly collectible, have a painted design instead of a woven one.

Carved wooden figures and masks are indigenous to the Kuba culture. Similar objects anchor the design of this room. An enormous mask covers the central portion of the wall opposite the doorway and becomes the main focal point. Smaller versions of the mask form shutters on the windows. The shutter masks can be opened to let the sun in and the music out. Even when the shutters are closed, the cutout facial features give an open feeling to the small studio.

To create your own mask design, look for traditional or contemporary African art designs in import stores, free-trade stores, and online. Adapt the pattern, simplifying it to make the construction easier and adjusting the size to fit your room.

### Jazz It Up

Red and orange are the main accent colors here. As focal-point features, the mask and shutters sport the largest amount of color. They immediately draw the eye and make the room feel anchored. Tissue-embellished candleholders and wall hangings repeat the warm colors in small doses to create unity. A painted border on the rug puts subtle pattern underfoot.

The candleholders (see *page 161*) are easy to duplicate and make a good color accent for any room. Colorful tissue paper is cut into squares and glued onto a glass cylinder in a geometric pattern until the glass is entirely covered. One or two final coats of diluted glue or matte decoupage medium seal the surface. Mark used red, brown, and ivory papers to pick up the room's main colors, but any three colors that harmonize with a room's color scheme would work.

Painting a sisal rug is a quick way to add personality to a ready-made item. Good-quality acrylic paint from a crafts store provides the best coverage. Mark used a 1-inch-wide brush to apply the paint in Kuba-inspired designs. It may take more than one coat for the color to pop. Practice curving designs on plain paper first to master the technique before committing to the rug.

---

**LEFT** The mask design was adapted to make these large wooden shutters, which have a simple hook latch to keep them closed. **OPPOSITE** Accessories in the room look like African artifacts, but some of them are easy do-it-yourself projects (see *page 165*).

# "He works really hard...and he needed a place where he can drum." – *Janice*

# The space takes a definite turn toward African design—a perfect match for a future conga drum player.

## Bring It On Home

A studio is a natural gathering place for both musicians and non-musicians, and a few touches of home make it even more inviting. A pillow-lined bench offers seating. The cutout designs on the back and the curved legs echo the Kuba cloth and mask patterns; the rubbed stain finish helps the bench blend with the elephant grass, wood, and stone background. A shelving unit with similar curves holds small percussion instruments and earthy accessories. Carved masks, baskets, and an assortment of vessels promote the multicultural look. Similar accessories for creating this look may be found at import stores, flea markets, free-trade stores, and ethnic fairs. (Free-trade stores help support developing countries by importing native arts and crafts and returning the profits to the workers.)

Hanging lamps made from rattan wastebaskets spotlight dark areas. This creative repurposing involves turning the wastebasket upside down and drilling a hole in the center of the bottom to receive the cord and fixture of a hanging lamp kit. (Lamp kits are available at home improvement centers and hardware stores.) Cowrie shells, glued onto the lamp and to basket edges, are more than a decorative element; they recall the fact that historically cowrie shells served as a form of currency in Africa and the South Pacific.

**OPPOSITE A rustic bookshelf was constructed from 1×12-inch pine boards. The end supports were cut to be narrower at the top and bottom. Baskets on the shelves were accented with shell borders. RIGHT This hanging lamp was made from a wastepaper basket.**

## Basket Lamp

1 To make the hanging lamp, select a slatted wastepaper basket large enough to provide ample space between the side of the basket and the lightbulb. Turn the wastepaper basket upside down and drill a hole in the center, making it just large enough to receive the electrical wiring. Using a hanging lamp kit, wire the basket according to the kit instructions.

2 Collect or buy small shells that are approximately the same size and kind. Hot-glue the shells to form a repeating diamond pattern around the center section of the basket. Use high-heat glue to ensure that the shells stay in place when the lamp is lit. To hang the lamp, use decorative hooks screwed into the ceiling joists or use ceiling anchors.

# Sweet
# Disco
# Alabama

## Designer Nadia Geller creates disco drama with punchy purple walls, a stand-up stage, and laser lights to surprise the boyfriend of Catherine Crosby, a former Miss Alabama.

*Before*

he challenge: Transform a boring Birmingham basement filled with bland, overstuffed furniture and blank white walls into a New York City disco-dream space with the latest in nightclub technology. And complete this makeover in less than 48 hours on a strict $1,500 budget. It's more than demanding—it's crazy!

But leave it up to designer Nadia Geller, host Evan Farmer, and carpenters Leslie Segrete and Andrew Dan-Jumbo to take on the challenge and succeed. They brought to life the vision of Catherine Crosby, a former Miss Alabama, who hoped to magically make over the space for her boyfriend, Tyler. According to Catherine, Tyler was a great support to her during her year as Miss Alabama, and this makeover was her way of saying thank you. To get Tyler out of the way, *While You Were Out* arranged a trip for him and his friend and business partner, Jeff.

Tyler's problem area was his basement, which he often used for social gatherings in his home. It was a large, uninviting room that communicated no real sense of purpose. The mismatched furniture lacked sophistication and visual continuity, and Catherine said that most guests found the squishy sofas so unappealing that they

preferred to stand rather than sit. Making matters worse, the overhead lighting cast strong shadows and was too harsh for relaxing or for evening parties.

### Zoned-Out Design

Open floor plans, such as undivided basements and lofts, work best when there are clearly defined areas within the larger space. Even though they may not have permanent walls or dividers, open floor plans can be divided by less permanent means, such as hanging draperies, fabric panels, or artwork. The creative placement of furniture, movable shelving, and screens can also subdivide a large room into smaller, more inviting areas.

Other less obvious ways to create zones within a larger area include raising or

This basement party room has been creatively divided to provide for both intimate and large-group activities. The same colors and upbeat styling throughout unify the large space.

VINYL RECORDS SPRAY PAINTED GOLD

SPANDEX STRETCHED OVER STRING LIGHTS

BLACK SOFA W/ VELVET BILLOWS

MIRRORED TILE TABLE MAKE-DO

# "Thankfully, I work with many skilled craftspeople; when we all put our heads together, crazy things can happen." — Leslie Segrete

lowering the floor or ceiling height, introducing rug or flooring changes, making color changes on the walls or ceiling, or using lighting in varying intensities.

For Tyler's room, Nadia implemented several of these methods. She used sheer draperies behind the futon to define the conversation area and provide more privacy and intimacy for small groups. Specialty lighting at the bar changes the mood in that zone and energizes it for upbeat conversations. The hanging light over the pool table emits a glow that washes over the tabletop and illuminates it for game playing. And in the stage and dance area, the carpet was removed and a more suitable floor of tile was installed, clearly marking the space for a different function.

## The Right Light

Lighting the basement was critical for defining the zones, but it was most important in creating atmosphere. Overhead lighting typically causes unattractive shadows and creates an unwelcoming glare that discourages relaxation. By installing a variety of general, task, and mood illumination, Nadia made the room much more interesting and inviting. With the addition of dimmer switches, the lighting levels can be raised or lowered, depending on the function of the zone and the type of gathering.

**OPPOSITE Old records spray-painted gold serve as an inexpensive wall treatment behind the bar. RIGHT Tyler's first initial marks his new dance floor. The tile is readily available and easy to install, and it comes in a wide array of colors (some colors must be special-ordered).**

Disco Dance Floor

1 Determine where to place the dance floor and mark off the area with a masking tape border. If possible, to eliminate cutting the tile, keep the dimensions of the installation area to feet and no inches. Map the area to be tiled on graph paper and plot where color changes (such as the T initial in this case) will be. Consider a checkerboard or border design as an alternative to the monogram.

2 Prepare the area to be tiled by removing the old carpet or flooring. Use the masking tape as a cutting guide. For carpet, use a metal ruler or straightedge and run the carpet knife next to it for a clean cut. After the old flooring has been removed, scrape off any glue residue, vacuum, and clean the floor thoroughly; allow it to dry.

3 Make snap lines to guide the placement of the tiles. Install the tiles according to manufacturer's directions, using the appropriate adhesive for non-self-adhesive tiles. (Keep the area well-ventilated and stay off the tiles for the suggested time period.) Trim the dance floor with transition floor strips suitable for the flooring materials used.

## Mosaic Coffee Table

1 Cut MDF (medium-density fiberboard) for the top of the coffee table. Wrap mirror squares (available from home-improvement centers) or old mirrors in layers of newspaper. Carefully hit the paper bundle with a hammer to break the mirrors. Try to break the mirrors so the pieces are of diverse sizes. (Caution: Wear safety glasses and heavy gloves when doing this project.)

If you are incorporating a variety of new lighting in a large room like this one, consider having a professional electrician install a control panel with separate dimmer switches for each of the zones. This lets you control all the light sources in the whole space from one spot, so adjustments can be made quickly, with an eye to the overall ambience.

While most rooms have general or overhead lighting, consider using other lights to better illuminate your space and add personality to the decor. For example, use lighting to highlight architectural features or paintings, to increase safety on a staircase, or to add drama in a bedroom or dining area.

Include a variety of light sources in the same room. Table lamps, uplights, lava lights, wall-mounted sconces, rope lighting, and hanging fixtures serve different functions and help define the decorating style of the room. Be on the lookout for creative ways to add lighting too: Nadia dressed the front of the bar in white mini-lights, which she hid behind a covering of heavy blue plastic. The effect is perfect for creating a big-city nightclub atmosphere.

### Groove Things

No room is complete without the proper accessories, and this one is no different. Because the room is designed to encourage people to get up and party, the accents must have a hip-and-happenin' style and be durable enough to hold up in a space that may experience heavy use.

RIGHT The mirror mosaic coffee table and acrylic coasters were projects designed by Nadia. OPPOSITE A gold sheer, hung from the ceiling, provides a backdrop for the futon sofa and creates a more intimate seating area.

"I just wanted to say thank you and give him a place that he could enjoy with his friends." —Catherine Crosby

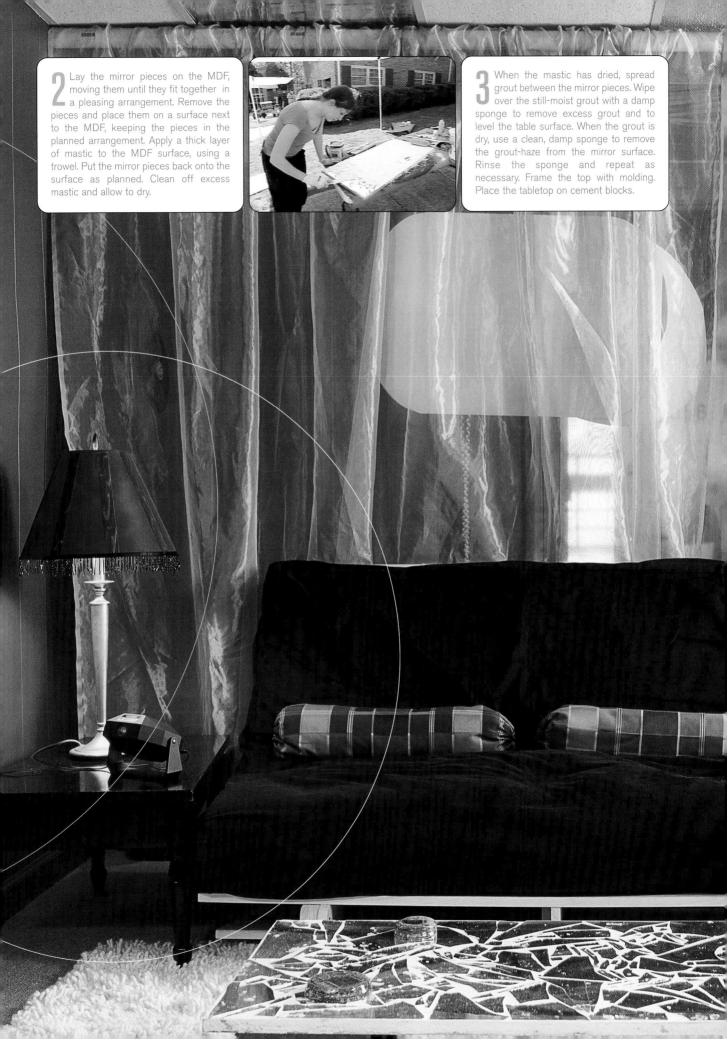

**2** Lay the mirror pieces on the MDF, moving them until they fit together in a pleasing arrangement. Remove the pieces and place them on a surface next to the MDF, keeping the pieces in the planned arrangement. Apply a thick layer of mastic to the MDF surface, using a trowel. Put the mirror pieces back onto the surface as planned. Clean off excess mastic and allow to dry.

**3** When the mastic has dried, spread grout between the mirror pieces. Wipe over the still-moist grout with a damp sponge to remove excess grout and to level the table surface. When the grout is dry, use a clean, damp sponge to remove the grout-haze from the mirror surface. Rinse the sponge and repeat as necessary. Frame the top with molding. Place the tabletop on cement blocks.

i eat glue

Nadia accessorized the room with items she and the team created specifically for this environment. For artwork behind the bar, she spray-painted old records gold and hung them close together. She also made a smashing mirror mosaic coffee table and, with Catherine's help, resin coasters that showcase some of Tyler's old ticket stubs.

The coasters are easy to make, but it's important to work in a well-ventilated area. Nadia and Catherine started with clear jars and poured a resin mixture into the bottom, along with a few silver beads. When the resin solution began to harden, the ticket stubs were carefully laid on top. A film of resin covered the tickets, so they look as if they're floating. When the resin was dry, the glass jars were carefully broken to release the coasters.

The well-planned details added just the right energy to spark the colorful walls, new dance floor and stage area, and freshly furnished zones to give the basement a good case of dance fever.

**LEFT A vibrant color scheme of purple and red adds energy to the space, perfect for a nightspot. Alternating rows of ceiling tiles are covered with lightweight, foil-like plastic to reflect the various lights. ABOVE Purchased ice-cube candleholders add drama to the space.**

"I like my rooms to have their own personalities that make their inhabitants comfortable and excited to be in the space." — *Nadia Geller*

# Index